Copyright © 2017 Charles Muhlenkamp. All Rights Reserved

Published by CORE Biz Systems, Puyallup, WA

No part of this publication may be reproduced, transmitted in any form or by any means, electronic, mechanical, photocopying, recording, scanning, or otherwise, except as permitted under section 107 or 108 of the 1976 United States Copyright Act, without either prior written permission of Publisher, or authorization through payments of the appropriate per-copy fee. Requests to the Publisher for permission should be sent to support@corebizsystems.com.

Limitation of Liability/Disclaimer of Warranty: Neither the publisher nor author represents or is affiliated with any product, service, or vendor mentioned in this book. While the publisher and author have used their best efforts in preparing this book, they make no representations or warranties with respect to the accuracy or completeness of the contents of this book and specifically disclaim any implied warranties of merchantability or fitness for a particular purpose. No warranty may be created or extended by sales representatives or written sales materials. The advice and strategies contained herein may not be suitable for your situation. You should consult with a professional where appropriate. Neither the publisher nor author shall be liable for any loss of profit or any other commercial damages, included but not limited to special, incidental, consequential, or other damages.

For general information on our other products and services, please go to www.corebizsystems.com.

Companies often claim to have trademark rights in the labels they apply to their products, and those claims may or may not be legally supportable. In all instances where the author or publisher is aware of a claim (whether valid or not), the product name appears in initial capital letters. Readers, however, should contact the appropriate companies for more complete information regarding trademark rights that may apply. No use of any trademark should be an indication of association, sponsorship, or approval by the trademark owners.

LegalShield is a registered trademark of Pre-Paid Legal Services.
GoSmallBiz is a registered trademark of FTSBN, Inc.

TABLE OF CONTENTS

Acknowledgement 1
Introduction 5
The State of Marketing Biz Plans and Small Biz Plans 17
Who the heck is Charlie Muhlenkamp 25
The System 49
The Foundation 57

    Role Acquisition 61
    Product Mastery 65
    Market Focus 73

The Sales Funnel 83

    Lead Generation 85
    Business Evaluation 91
    Getting Them Started 97

Momentum 101

    Solutions and Results 103
    Referral Acquisition 107
    Building Clientele 113

The Floodgates 117
Breaking Free of a Total State of Training Overwhelm 123
How to Win at This 129
The CORE Method 139
The Next Step 151

ACKNOWLEDGEMENTS

I would like to start by saying this book has been prepared for you at great personal and monetary expense in developing and compiling this information over the years. The information contained in this book did not come from theory or reading a training manual. The information contained in this book came from years of actual field work, trial and error, and testing in the small business marketplace. Actual work in real life applications were used to develop a proven system. A system which will eliminate the need for you to sacrifice the time, money, and impact on your family it cost those who went before you to figure all this out. You can work through this book and immediately benefit from the information presented.

This book is dedicated to the pioneers of the Small Business Division. Through their sacrifice, willingness to share, and desire to help others you have the incredible opportunity available to you today. I would personally like to thank the following leaders for their contribution to the small business division and for creating, cultivating, and making marketing Small Biz Plans the incredible opportunity that it is today:

- Lisa Bueno, Former Top Small Business Producer
- Nick and Gale Serba, Former Marketing Director for the Small Biz Program, Platinum 3 Executive Directors, Million Dollar Income Earners, and Millionaire Club Members
- Mr. Fran Tarkenton, Owner of GoSmallBiz
- The late, Mr. Harland Stonecipher, founder of Pre-Paid Legal Services
- Mr. Jeff Cordle, Formerly at GoSmallBiz
- Mr. Will Adams, Tarkenton Financial
- The Staff at GoSmallBiz and LegalShield
- Mr. John Sanchez
- Ace and Gina Fair, Platinum Executive Directors, Millionaire Club Members
- Mr. George Wilkinson
- Mr. Dan Stacy

- and the many other folks that have helped and contributed along the way.

Through the vision, leadership, willingness to teach, coach, and share their experience and knowledge, these people have helped make the Small Business Opportunity what it is today.

I want to thank Crystal for believing in my vision and my dreams. The encouragement and support she has provided has made this book possible.

I want to thank Freda Carda for being my Counselor and my guide through one of the most difficult times in my life.

I want to thank my son, Charlie Jr, for being a sounding board and for having wisdom and vision beyond his years.

Lastly, but certainly not least, I would like to thank my Mom for being my greatest supporter throughout the years. Her years of hard work and dedication has been a shining example to me.

Without all these people, this book would not have been possible.

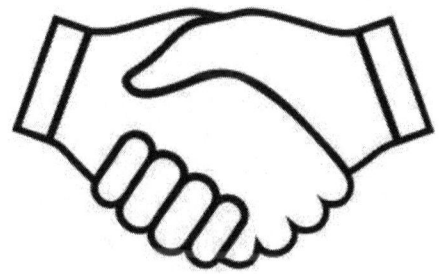

INTRODUCTION

This book is specifically for LegalShield Associates who want to generate above average results marketing Biz Plans and SmallBiz Plans. It's for Associates who would like to work their business as a full-time sole source of income they can count on and leave their jobs to pursue their business career. It's for Associates who want to CRUSH IT marketing Biz Plans and SmallBiz Plans. In short, it's for Associates who want to **BREAK FREE to Full-Time Income Marketing Biz Plans.**

Have you ever looked at the Leader Board and asked how certain people make it to the top while most struggle at the bottom? Is it luck or is it knowing all the right people? No, it's because those people at the top of the Leader Board are doing it differently than everyone else and you can also.

The problem is the world has changed and Traditional Training has not kept pace. What worked 40, 50, even 60 years ago when Amway was started does not work today.

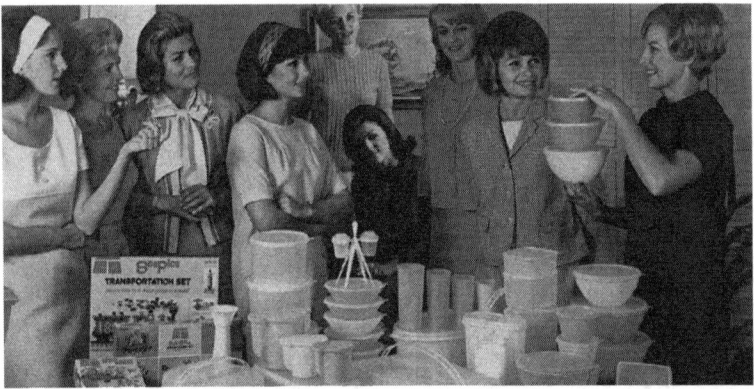

Back then the "in home meeting" craze was just getting started. Back then you were told to, "make a list" so you could invite everyone you know to your "in home meeting." Back then you were told to "follow your dollar" so you could use the money you spend with other people as leverage to get them to sit down with you and buy your product. Do these things sound familiar? This is right out of the Traditional Network Marketing Playbook created back in the late 50's. Back then you were also told to "go walk your community", go "door-to-door", or in other words, "cold call" to share your services. The difference between today and back then is back then, walking your community, door-to-door sales, and cold calling were, accepted methods of getting the word out regarding your products.

But today, things have changed. Most people are hip to these methods and avoid it like the plague. Back then many businesses were privately owned by a local merchant. Today, more and more local businesses are owned by corporations and the person running them is a manager who has no authority to purchase what you have to offer. Most associates today just don't do enough business with local, privately owned businesses to get their Biz Plan sales off the ground to generate consistent income.

If you're reading this book, you've probably already discovered these methods don't work effective in today's B2B, Small Business Marketplace to generate consistent.

In today's world people are super busy. Small Business Owners in this market space are trying to wear multiple hats to cut overhead and remain competitive. Because of this they don't take time to visit with door-to-door salespeople and they don't want to be sold, but they want to buy. What I mean by this is they don't want to be sold things they don't need. However, they are more than willing to buy things they do need. Today, Small Business Owners avoid the high-pressure salesperson at all costs. Often before you can even get a word out of your mouth to let the business owner know who you are, they are already saying "I'm not interested". You think to yourself, how do they know they are not interested when I haven't had the opportunity to present what I have to offer? They know because they've spotted you a mile off using the same tired, overused methods which have been around for over 60-years and are still being taught in the Traditional Training, Make a list, Follow Your Dollar, and Go Walk Your Community. Today's business owner doesn't have, or want to take the time to hear your scripted sales presentation for something they don't believe they need. They can spot the sale coming a mile off and avoid putting themselves in a situation of being pressured into purchasing something, or wasting their precious time needed to make their business work and earn a profit.

In today's world, the successful associate marketing Biz Plans at the top of the leader board have brought their marketing, sales methods, and techniques up-to-date. They're able to connect with business owners as equals, business owner to business owner. They're able to lead the business owner through a sales process where the business owner comes to the realization on their own they need what the associate has to offer and wants to purchase the product. They don't follow the Traditional Training of getting tools in the marketplace, sharing features and benefits, hoping someone will see something they need. Instead, they discover what the business owner needs and offers solutions.

Remember the movies where the submarine is trying to avoid the surface ship? Movies like "Hunt for Red October" with Sean Connery and Alec Baldwin, "Crimson Tide" with Denzel Washington and Gene Hackman, or "U-571" with Matthew McConaughey and Jon Bon Jovi. In these movies, the submarine was underwater and the surface ship was trying to destroy it.

You could hear the sound of the surface ship pinging away with sonar trying to find them. Then you see the surface ship start dropping depth charges. You would see the depth charges sinking into the ocean. Then they would show the inside of the submarine and the men would be looking up as though they could see the depth charges coming towards them. Next, there were underwater explosions and the submarine would shake and start leaking water. The men would rush out of the compartment, force the door close behind them and seal it to prevent the sub from sinking. Then they would rush to the next compartment and close the door behind them as the depth charges continued to explode. Finally, the sub fires its torpedo which hits and sinks the ship. The submarine has won and our heroes in the submarine are safe.

Today's sales process is like this timeless story.

As you complete each step of today's sales process you bring your prospect with you to the next compartment, close the door behind you and seal it so the prospect cannot run back to the previous compartment or step. You bring the prospect along with you through each step of the process, developing rapport and understanding, to allow them to come to the conclusion on their own they need what you are offering, the Biz Plan with GoSmallBiz add-on or the SmallBiz Plan. They sell themselves. This is today's sales model and you won't hear this taught in Traditional Training.

I'm Charlie Muhlenkamp and I started out just like you. I was trying to make my business work and generate consistent income I could count on to pay bills. I was desperately working to implement the Traditional Training into my business but it just wasn't working. I realized it wasn't working because the system being taught was antiquated. It was missing key elements I needed to generate consistent income and scale my business marketing biz plans. But, what we discovered next changed our business and propelled us to a National Top Small Biz Plan producer in less than 8 months. What we discovered completely changed our lives and it has changed the lives of other associates who I have taught this to. Some have gone on to be National Top Producers and trainers today. So, I know by using the information contained in this book you can do it as well.

If you've picked up this book and you're not an Independent LegalShield Associate, but what I'm sharing makes sense to you and you want to join the cause and help rebuild main street America by supporting Small Business Owners, I welcome you. If you want to help Small Business Owners grow and protect their businesses by giving them access to real business solutions and make a full-time income doing it, you're reading the right book. Read through this book, consume the information, and if everything you read makes sense to you and you're ready and willing to invest the time and money to build a solid home based business for you and your family then go to www.corebizsystems.com/getstartednow and I'll put you in contact with a LegalShield Associate who will help you get started. The associate will work with you to help you accomplish your hopes and dreams while helping Small Business Owners accomplish theirs. But, you must be willing to show up and do the work, this is not a get rich scheme. This is a real business opportunity.

In this book, I'm going to show you a simple one-page step-by-step strategy I used to become a National Top Producer and Top Producers use today to generate consistent, predictable, full-time income. It's also helping people who work their business on a spare-time or part-time level generate additional income for themselves and their family. I'm also going to show you how you can customize this system and strategy to your exact availability, circumstances, and marketplace, so you can put it to use in your business right away without information overwhelm. I will show you how to eliminate the guess work, stress, and frustration of trying to figure it all out on your own so you can market Biz Plans with the GoSmallBiz add-on, and/or SmallBiz Plans as a full-time, consistent, and predictable income. Sound good?

Perfect! Let's go...

"Is this for you?"

I get asked this question a lot because generating consistent income from personal sales production goes against the constant drum beat the Traditional Recruiting Training teaches of recruit, recruit, recruit and don't get it out of order. So, it goes back to a choice. Follow the Traditional Training the masses are using to get the traditional results most people are getting, or **Break Free** and accomplish the income level you want from your business where you can generate consistent, predictable income you can live on and pursue your dreams. There is certainly a time and a place for recruiting and I will share that with you later in this book. But you have to be able to make money at this to sustain your business while you're building a team.

This proven system works for full-time, part-time, and spare-time associates and in this book I am going to show you how to utilize the information for each of these business models. It works regardless of your age, gender or experience level. I work with single Moms and single Dads, senior citizens, men and women of different ethnicities and backgrounds, and men and women young and more seasoned all working to build solid businesses which generate consistent income. The bottom line is, this just works and it will work for you.

But the more important question than, "Is this for you?" is, are you actively working your business? Are you generating consistent income? Are you looking to take your business to a new level? The key question here is, are you working your business? The reason I ask is because the information contained in this book is not a "get rich quick" scheme. What I'm going to share with you works so amazingly well that it could be used by individuals who are looking for a fast buck, but are not willing to do the follow up work to bring value to their clients and treat this like a real business. If, that's you, please put this book down and walk away. The memberships will cancel off, you will suffer huge chargebacks, and you will give LegalShield and other LegalShield Associates who are trying to build solid businesses a bad name in the process.

There are also a lot of associates out there who are what I refer to as, "spectator." They say they want to be successful but they're looking for the shortcut which will allow them to have success without putting in the work required. What I know to be true is, you must pay full retail for success. No one achieves lasting success without it. My good friend, Ace Fair, who is a Millionaire Club Member says, "If it's easy, it's sleazy" and he's right. You can make that purchase by investing your own time and money to gain your own experience through trial and error which can be quite costly in time and money and most quit before they figure it all out. You can also make that full retail purchase by gaining the experience of someone else who paid the full retail price. The point is if you're spectating, looking for a shortcut to success that doesn't require work, again, this book is probably not for you.

Who this book is for is the honest, hardworking associate who wants to build a solid business which will generate consistent predictable income. It's for the associate who wants to work with business owners to help them grow and protect their business.

They're in it for the long haul, wants or needs to scale their business fast, and just needs a clear, step-by-step path to success. If that's you, then what I'm about to share with you is going to be a pleasant surprise from the Traditional Training you get everywhere else.

This book contains a proven system and I've shared this information with hundreds of associates. Some have taken this information and applied it in their business, and as I said, some have become Top Producers and trainers today. However, those associates are not typical. Most associates never implement this information, or any other information for that matter, and fail in their business. This book is for associates looking for a step-by-step process they can implement in their business quickly to increase their income to the level they desire. It's for associate who want to consistently qualify for Performance Club. It's for associates who want to take control of their income through their own activities, which are the only activities you really have control over, and are willing and able to do what's required to be successful. I know when I got started in this business I would have loved to have the information I'm going to share with you. It would have dramatically accelerated our business growth and income.

So why is this information different from what you get everywhere else?

Because I'm not going to talk about all the things you hear through Traditional Training like make a list, follow your dollar, and go walk your community (cold call). Some of the names have changed over the years but the activities are the same and doesn't work effectively in today's world. If you've done these things already, you know what I'm talking about and it's not what really matters when marketing Biz Plans and SmallBiz Plans for consistent income.

What I'm going to share with you is new, cutting edge systems and techniques you probably haven't seen before, and is completely opposite of what Traditional Trainings are pushing you to do. Best of all, this system can be customized to your exact situation, availability, and marketplace. I've spent over 30 years and tons of time and money learning all this stuff and pulling it all together into one step-by-step system to help you shorten your learning curve so hopefully you'll think it's pretty cool.

My goals for creating this book were simple:

1) Show you a brand-new strategy you can use to launch or scale your Biz Plan and SmallBiz Plan marketing efforts immediately in your business.
2) Discover an effective way to get in front of your ideal client prospects without cold calling or humiliating yourself.
3) Walk you through a Biz Plan marketing plan that can take you from zero to consistent, predictable income without all the information and training overwhelm, this is super simple.

And if that's not enough, I'm also going to give you access to some frameworks and a simple one-page sales strategy to help you implement this system in your business. I'm also going to give you access to some bonus training videos to help you shorten your learning curve.

Go to the link below to download the frameworks I'll be teaching in this book:

https://corebizsystems.com/forms

If you purchased this book during the Pre-Launch you should have received links to the bonus videos. If you purchase this book from Amazon, email a copy of your receipt from Amazon to bonusvideos@corebizsystems.com and we will send you the links to the bonus training videos.

As you read through this book, I would encourage you to have a note pad and jot down notes and highlight information you want to come back to. I want you to use this book as a workbook and a guide to launch your Biz Plan and SmallBiz Plan marketing efforts. So, underline, highlight, and write in the margins to help you absorb and use this information. I've taken over 4,000 associates through this information and I know how transformational it can be. I also suggest you read straight through this book and then circle back around for a second read. It will help you to absorb the information and get a greater understanding of the content. As you circle back around for your second read, you will understand things at a much higher level. I want to make sure you get full benefit from the information I'm going to share. This is like going to a movie a second or third time. Each time you go back and watch the movie, even though it's the exact same movie, you see things differently and notice things you didn't see the first or second time through. The information contained in this book will be the same way. As you read and re-read, apply the information and re-read, you will understand the information at different levels as you implement and progress in your business. This is the transformation I talked about earlier. This book will almost take on a life of its own as it teaches you and unlocks new dimensions of discovery and understanding at each step of this transformation.

Lastly, I challenge you to implement what you'll learn in this book. I challenge you to go beyond yourself and take up this cause of helping business owners grow and protect their businesses. I challenge you to work to generate the income you desire by helping others succeed in their businesses and I challenge you get to the top of the leader board and continue to show other associates it's possible.

THE STATE OF MARKETING BIZ PLANS and SMALLBIZ PLANS

The Legal Transformation Institute shares there is roughly 23 million small businesses in the US. They put the potential untapped market for Legal Services at about $45 Billion, with a B. Infodesk also shows huge grow expected in the Business Consulting sectors. It's unfortunate with such a HUGE marketplace and such a tremendous income opportunity, very few associates are able to generate consistent, predictable income marketing Biz Plans or SmallBiz Plans.

There are 23 million small businesses in the US. Roughly 7 million did not seek the help of a lawyer when presented with a significant legal event. Those that did get legal help, report that they spend on average $7600 per year. This creates an untapped market (the 7 million who avoid lawyers) equal to roughly **$45bb**.

An Uptick in Hiring Consultants
One especially welcome trend may be the increase in the hiring of consultants within 2016. The hiring restrictions of the recession era are easing, as evidenced by a survey of 23 consultancies by Prism. All of the consulting firms surveyed stated that they would be increasing their hiring in 2017.

However, that's to be expected without a method of marketing which allows for consistent predictable results. An associate cannot invest their time and money to market the plans without some assurance they will get a return on investment. The Traditional Training teaches the average associate to get tools into the marketplace. Associates are encouraged to make a list of anyone they know who owns a business. However, in most cases the average associate personally knows very few people who owns a business they would feel comfortable talking to.

The Traditional Training teaches the average associate to get tools into the marketplace by following their dollar and using the relationship they have with a business as leverage to pressure the business owner into sitting down with them and purchasing a plan. However, with the transition from locally owned businesses to corporate owned locally managed businesses, few associates have access to the actual business owners they are trying to sign up using this method.

The Traditional Training teaches the average associates to get tools into the marketplace by "walking their community" or cold calling on businesses in their local marketplace. They're encouraged to walk into businesses, introduce themselves as their LegalShield Representative, the one they would purchase LegalShield services through, leave them a tool, and set an appointment to follow up with them at some future date about purchasing the service. The problem with this is most associates, and people in general, would rather die than cold call. Those who muster up the courage to venture out and give it a shot, find the huge rejection rate horrendous and quickly stop doing this activity.

Have associates had some success with these approaches? Of course. However, the success is so limited even these people quit using them after only a short period of time. Just look up the people being featured on corporate calls on the leader board and see how many plans they're actually marketing. In nearly all cases it's shocking how few plans have been sold and yet the person is still being featured on a call and sharing what they're doing as something which works. My rub with this is it gives that method, which in most cases isn't working effectively, credibility and the unsuspecting associate listening to the call believes it works, goes out and tries it, and when it doesn't work they quit trying to market Biz Plans because in their mind marketing Biz Plans doesn't work. Nothing could be farther from the truth. It works if you work it correctly using proven systems.

Why do these Traditional Methods continue to be taught if they're so ineffective? Because these methods are simple to do, don't require a lot of training or practicing, and when applied with massive activity (hundreds or thousands of associates) doing them provides the result corporate needs to continue to be profitable. Sound horrible? Not really. Keep in mind the Federal Trade Commission reported that most direct sales reps will never make money in their business and most will quit within 6-months or at least as representatives. This method of marketing, which has been around since before the 60's, is designed to get the average associate, the masses, to engage in a simple activity which will in the greater scheme of things allow for memberships to be sold and people to be recruited. However, on the individual associate level, it's not an effective approach which will allow the individual associate a method to effectively market Biz Plans or SmallBiz Plans at a full-time, consistent, or predictable income level. With a predictable method, you do activity "X", "Y" number of times, and you WILL get "Z" result. Without this predictable formula, no one can use the method. It's a gamble every time and you know how that turns out. Lot of money in, little money out. It's how the casinos stay in business and afford their lavished buildings.

If you take a moment to look over the leader board in your back office you will see how few Biz Plans are being sold by the average associate. When I saw this, I knew clearly something had to change. After trying the Traditional Method and getting the same, or similar results most associates were getting, I knew a different method was required to get the results I was looking for and needed. That's when a System was born.

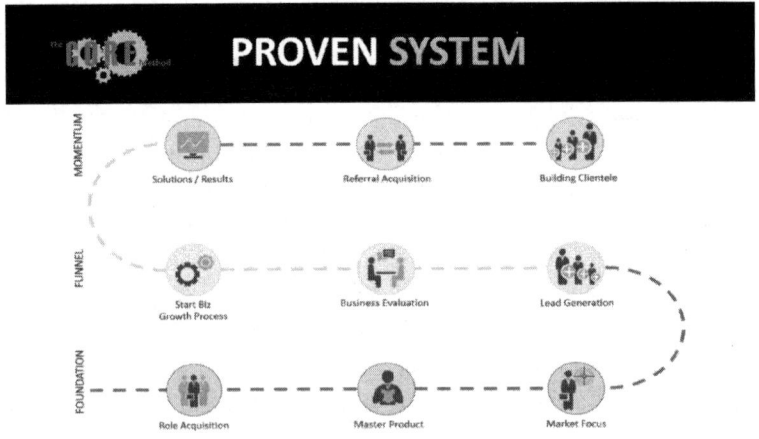

The positive thing is there is a different way of doing things which produces predictable results and can be scaled to the full-time income level and beyond and we've proven it. ==We discovered a 9-Step system which turns the Traditional Training upside down and brings the associate who wants to build a solid business and income into the modern times.== It is a system where a business owner will want to sit down with you. As they progress through the system with you, they come to their own conclusion they want to purchase the Biz Plan or SmallBiz Plan from you, allowing you to be able to do this and have success at it.

Who wins and who loses in today's Small Business Marketplace? Simply put, the associate who loses is the associate who never discovers this new approach to marketing Biz Plans and SmallBiz Plans, or who cannot break free from the Traditional Training.

The associates who win are the associates who understand there is a new more effective approach which will generate consistent predictable income marketing Biz Plans and SmallBiz Plans. They invest the time and effort to master this new system, apply it in their business, and work to build a solid business and income.

When we first started in LegalShield, Pre-Paid Legal back then, the system I'm going to share in this book didn't exist. We were told to put a survey, which was the 12 questions from the back of the GoSmallBiz Directory Listing form at the time, with Fran Tarkenton's Protect and Grow cassette (just dated myself) into an envelope. Our trainer suggested we drop the packet off at businesses and ask the business owner to listen to the tape, fill out the survey, and we would be back in a few days to pick up the survey. We purchased a couple boxes of the cassettes from GoSmallBiz, put the envelopes together and hit the streets. However, nearly every time we would go back, the business owner had done nothing with the package. We had the same experience dropping off other tools in hopes of a sit down on our return. We were spending tons of time, and a lot of money getting tools into the market with no return.

We needed to make this work because we were trying to work our business as our sole source of income and we had to quickly start generating different results than what we had been getting. I shared our situation with our certification trainer and he said, "Charlie, if you're financially embarrassed you need to just start going door-to-door." Does that sound familiar? They call it "Go Walk Your Community" now. However, we needed to make it work so we took his advice. I had also been listening to a Jim Rohn training where he shared, "what he lacked in experience he would make up in volume." So, that's exactly what we were going to do. With no system in place, just walking our community, we earned $2,500 in the next month. We got the different result we were looking for and quite frankly needed. However, the work was not effective, income was still inconsistent, and the rejection level was extremely high.

We continued to experiment with different tools, different approaches, talked to our up-line Gold ED, got some prospecting advice and read tons of books to create the system I'm going to share in this book. Over the next 8 months we went from zero to a National Top Small Biz Producer allowing us to create consistent income and work while our kids were in school.

Is there work involved? Absolutely! No worthwhile, long-term business activity which will provide you with the income you want can be obtained without it. Is there training involved? Absolutely! If there wasn't additional knowledge and experience required, you wouldn't be reading this book and you would have already been marketing Biz Plans and SmallBiz Plans at the level you desire. The nice thing is, the information is now available for you to make this happen in your life and your business if you're willing to learn, implement, and apply the information I'm going to be sharing in this book.

WHO THE HECK IS CHARLIE MUHLENKAMP

Who the heck am I and why do you care? Maybe you don't.

You see I'm no one special. But, I'm going to give you the world's shortest biography because I believe it applies directly to you and your business. I'm going to share some things I found out through this journey we call life. It will help you jump forward and avoid the missteps and pitfalls that kill so many associate's hopes and dreams, and I want you to clearly see if I can do this, you can do this also.

Shortly after I lost everything in a previous brick and mortar business I had purchased, I was at a Doctor's appointment with my ex-wife. I was sitting there in the waiting room while she was in with the Doctor looking at the magazine table and noticed a "Success from Home" magazine. I picked it up and started reading the article on the featured business, Pre-Paid Legal Services.

I had left a successful career in corporate America to pursue my dreams of becoming an entrepreneur. However, I bet on the wrong horse. I had purchased a brick and mortar business which was in distress thinking I could quickly turn it around and make it my dream business. I invested everything I owned, and some I borrowed, only to lose it all. So, I was looking for something, and I was ready to dive in with both feet as soon as I found it.

As I read the article on LegalShield, Pre-Paid Legal back then, I connected to the article in a powerful way. The need in the marketplace and the company mission to provide equal access really resonated with me. You see my mom had been a Paralegal Secretary for 25 years as I was growing up and then went to work for Boeing in their Military division working on military contracts where she eventually retired. In addition to the understanding I learned from her experiences over the years of the need for legal access as a business owner, I had run companies where having access to an attorney was vital to our success. All the companies I had worked for and helped run either had an attorney on retainer so I could speak to them whenever I needed to or had an in-house attorney which gave me the same access. When I ventured out on my own, I didn't have this kind of access and it cost me dearly. Because of these experiences I knew the value and the need for such a service. I asked the receptionist if I could have the magazine and she thankfully said yes.

I contacted the person whose name and number was on a label attached to the outside cover of the magazine and I got started. If nothing else, this proves even the most ineffective use of a tool, done often enough will generate a result, supporting the Traditional Training at some level, or does it? I'll talk about in a minute.

Back to my story, I was told to get certified in everything, so I did. I took Small Biz Certification, Group Certification, and CDLP Certification. But, it was the Small Biz Plan opportunity I was most interested in because of my background. I thought marketing Biz Plans seemed like a logical progression and focus for me. However, my up-line said, "No, what we do is recruit. Everything else is a distraction."

My up-line Executive Director (ED) was one of the leaders at the front of the room at the largest briefing and systems training in the Los Angeles Marketplace at the time. He was the one driving the BMW, wearing the nice suits, and from what I understood from his brief bio he shared at each briefing, lived in a very nice, very expensive neighborhood. He seemed to have it all going on.

On the other hand, I was the new guy on the block. Struggling to pay bills and support my family at the time. So, I said, "if he is having success recruiting and is having that success getting tools out in the marketplace, getting people to the Briefings, Systems Training, and Super Saturday's, then I'll do the same things".

He said, "get on tools auto-ship". So, I did, even though we couldn't really afford it at the time.

He said, "get tools out into the marketplace". So, I did.

The Traditional Training at the time was sharing if you get 7 "Success from Home" magazines in the marketplace, properly done, this activity would generate a sale or a new recruit, "on average." I did the math, knew how much I needed to make, calculated how many tools I needed in the marketplace to get there and I went to work.

I would get up in the morning, go to my local gas station and walk up to people offering them the magazine in exchange for a phone number so I could follow up with them and see what they thought of it. The script the Traditional Training was teaching. Day after day I would do this religiously.

We were also applying the 3' Rule taught by Traditional Training. Anyone within 3' should be contacted. At the time, my ex-wife was working a day job at a local car dealership and as customers would come in she would talk to them about the business opportunity and/or the family plan. We had also made the Traditional List of everyone we knew and were contacting everyone in our family who would listen, and were begging them to join our business.

Enter Murphy's Law. Anything that can go wrong, will go wrong. Our numbers didn't match the corporate numbers, something was wrong. While we were making some sales using the Traditional Training methods, it was not enough to sustain us and we were falling further behind on our bills.

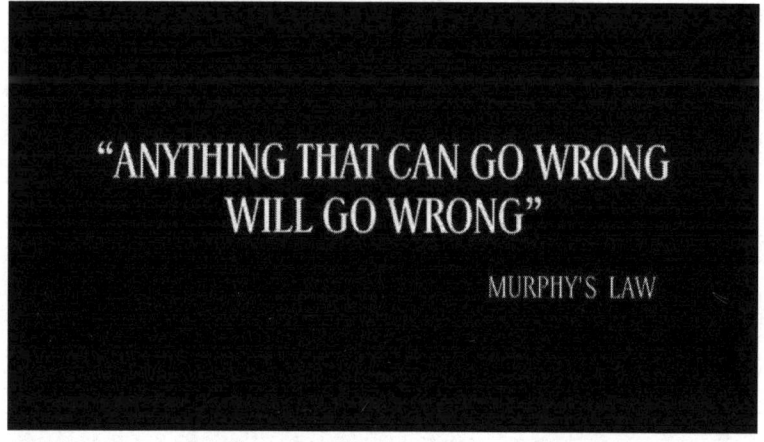

I talked to my up-line ED about this and he said just keep doing what you're doing, "Follow the System", the Traditional Training. So, I would plug in my Jim Rohn and my Jeff Olsen CDs and listen to them repeatedly to try and find what I was missing. I repeatedly asked my up-line ED to come out into the field with me and show me what I was doing wrong. However, we couldn't seem to make a connection and nothing seemed to be working as presented. The number of people who responded positively to a tool was far less than the number being presented by the Traditional Training. When I finally had an interested party, and tried to find one of my up-lines to do a 3-way phone call no one was available. I was becoming extremely frustrated.

Even though we had gotten to the level of Director by recruiting everyone in the organization, I wasn't making enough money to pay my bills and we continued to fall behind. No one was doing anything. I'm sure you can relate to this.

Out of shear harassment I finally got my up-line ED to go out into the field with me to help me figure out what I was doing wrong. What happened next first shocked me, then devastated me, and then made me angry. I watched my up-line ED walk up to people without a tool, share a script that hadn't been taught at weekly events to get 10 phone numbers in less than 20 minutes. I was standing there watching with my mouth hanging open. I couldn't believe it. I asked him, "What was that?" He shared everyone does it differently and that was how he did it. He went on to tell me one of the other "leaders", who was up front and teaching each week at the weekly briefing and system training, just passes out business cards. Whoever called him back is who he worked with. I was upset to put it mildly.

I was spending money on tools I couldn't afford, or rather shouldn't have afforded because that's what I was being taught. I was trying to be "CORE" and follow the Traditional Training, but that wasn't the system the leaders were using to accomplish their level of success. This was when I realized what was being taught during the Traditional Training was not what top producers and many leaders were doing. This is when I realized the Traditional Training is for those other associates, the average associates, who in most cases will never do anything. It is designed to try to get those associates to do something, anything, to get a few sales and recruit a few people before they drop out so the company can continue to grow and stay in business. Completely understandable and logical. However, I wasn't one of those other associates, the average associates. I needed this to work and produce consistent, predictable income or I couldn't do this for my sole source of income. And at this point, I needed it to work NOW!!! I would imagine, since you're still reading this book, you're not one of those other associates either?

The worst part was right around this time, because I wasn't making enough money I had fallen so behind on my bills, my cars were repossessed, and I had to move my family in with our parents. I walked out the front door of our house to see our car which was parked out in front, sitting on a tow truck. I ran to the back of our house where there was a gated parking to find our other car already gone. While my kids watched, the Repo man was kind enough to allow me to get our belongings out of the car.

As you're reading this you may be saying, I can totally relate to that, or you might be saying, "that would be the end of it for me, I would have been done." Well, it was a moment of despair and embarrassment. But, it's not the end to the story. It was the final straw, a turning point, a defining moment in my life and business. Thankfully, I didn't quit. As my car was being towed down the street, and I watched it go around the corner and disappear, something Jim Rohn had said on one of his CDs struck me like a ton of bricks. He said, "You must face the numbers." I thought, I must face the numbers? Then I remember what he said after that, "Your numbers will tell you everything." "How to amend your errors and set a better sail." He was right, I had to face the facts. What I was doing wasn't working. I was just wasting time and money. It didn't matter if I did it a thousand more times, it just wasn't working. At that moment I decided I was going to follow my heart and not worry about what others, or my up-line was going to say. If I was going to do this for a living, I had to make enough money, enough profits, to make it work.

I borrowed the money to get my cars back and started looking for how to pull this all together and get moving in the right direction. About this time my up-line insisted I go to convention in Oklahoma City (OKC).

He said he had a seat on the team bus for me, a ticket to the event, and a room once I got there. I thought maybe I could find what I was looking for there, so I conceded and went.

I had been on lots business trips before with companies I had worked for and managed. While I never went first class, we flew to our destinations, stayed in our own rooms, and took care of business. Quite a difference from what I was about to be exposed to.

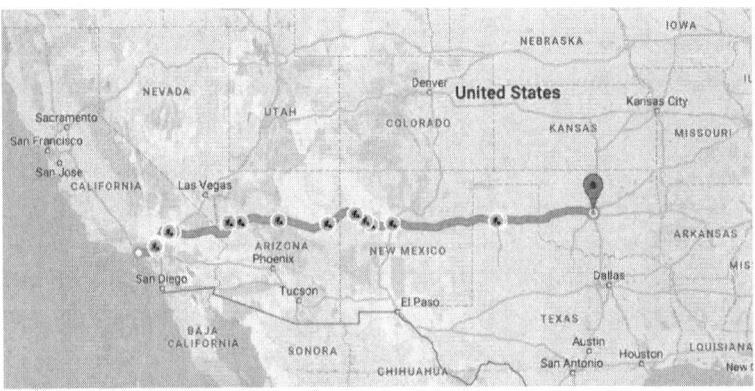

First, I had never gone cross country on a bus of any kind. So, that was a unique experience in and of itself. The 24-hour bus ride from Los Angeles to OKC was full of overly excited young adults, mostly in their late teens and early twenties, who stayed up all night. When we stopped at a truck stop in the middle of nowhere, everyone immediately jumped up, got into their bags, grabbed business cards and rushed into the McDonalds to grab some food. By the time I got up to the counter, the poor guy taking orders had a stack of business cards from everyone that repeatedly tried to recruit him. Walking back to the bus, I saw associates climbing on trucks which were driving through the parking lot to "expose' the truck drivers. I thought to myself, this is not the vision.

If you've never taken the team bus to a convention I highly recommend you do it at least once. <u>The experience will cause you to do whatever you must to never have to do that again.</u> By the next convention a year later, my ex-wife and I rented an A6 Audi and drove ourselves to convention, stopping at the half way point each way for a good night's sleep in a hotel.

Because of our financial condition at the time, we didn't have a lot of money to be spending on a trip to convention. So, I got on the bus with a loaf of bread and a jar of peanut butter in my bag and $100 in my pocket to last me the entire trip. To make matters worse, that was the year it snowed the first day of convention and I was dressed for California weather. I know this all sounds hard to believe, but it's true. That's what I had available and what I needed to do to get there so I could find what I was looking for. I was on a mission, so I was more than willing to do it. My Dad was a Marine and he taught us from an early age to deal with what we had, to adapt and overcome. So, that's what I did.

When we got to the hotel, I was in for yet another surprise. The room was a shared room with two queen beds and six guys. By the end of the first day the tub looked like someone had put mud in the bottom. But again, I didn't care. I was there for one reason, to find my way forward, and sure enough, my path forward was shared during two segments. The first segment was when Ace and Gina Fair were sharing the Small Biz Opportunity. When they finished with their segment I told my sponsor, "that's what I was going to do." To which he started heckling me. He said, "oh sure, you're going to be the next Ace Fair," and then laughed. I didn't care, I was laser focused by this point. However, within a very short period of time I would share the stage with Ace and his awesome wife Gina at convention and GoSmallBiz Boot Camps talking and training on the Small Biz opportunity. Surprisingly, once we got back home and my sponsor's Biz Plan overrides started to role in the heckling quickly stopped and was replaced by, "go boy go." Imagine that. Results are the name of the game.

The second segment which sealed the deal was done by Russel Peden where he was training on "Maximizing the Compensation Plan." As I watched him share his presentation everything became clear, I knew exactly what I needed to do. I said if they can make that kind of money marketing family plans, can you imagine what I could make marketing biz plans. It was the information and inspiration I needed to set my sail, and set it I did.

When I got back I sought out my up-line Silver ED for advice, jumping past my up-line ED who kept preaching the Traditional Training and to recruit, recruit, recruit. I was hoping to get in contact with someone in my up-line who could help me get started marketing Biz Plans. When I shared what I wanted to do he said, "I don't sell Small Biz Plans, I just recruit." I thought, here we go again. But what he said next was music to my ears. He said, "But I know who might be able to help you." Turns out our up-line Gold ED was doing Group Sales and he thought he could help me. He scheduled a call and from that call I was invited to my Up-line Gold ED's beautiful home on the cliffs above San Clemente.

Using my past business experience, I put together a business plan and some numbers I wanted his advice on. When he saw what I wanted to do he said, "If you could do this, the numbers would be much more than what you have in this plan." I was happy with what I had so I was very happy with what he said. But then the meeting took a strange twist. His wife looked at what I wanted to do and she said, "That's not the system, that's not CORE. You should just follow the system." As I looked at her, it was like everything was going in slow motion. I was thinking to myself, did she just say follow the Traditional Training and Traditional System which isn't working for us, that can't be right. Thankfully I ignored her advice. I had made a choice and a commitment to make my business work for my family, and I was going to use Biz Plans as the vehicle to generate the income and the lifestyle I wanted my family to have.

So, we went to work. Now, things didn't happen overnight. There was no system in place for marketing Biz Plans, and everyone who was marketing Biz Plans were doing it differently. I knew if this was going to work and be duplicated by others, a system had to be developed and I needed to figure it out. It was definitely a process and we were still struggling financially.

While we were figuring this out, we needed money for gas and food. So, to generate extra income, I thought we could do some recycling to get some extra money together. I went around to local bars and pizza places and asked them what they did with their empty glass beer bottles? The ones who said they just throw them away, I asked if I could leave a plastic bin and they could put the bottles in it for us. I would come by at the end of the day, or every other day depending on the volume, take the bottles and give them a clean bin. Most were happy to do this for us and I would run around and pick up all the bins, take them to the local recycling company for cash. The cash allowed us to put fuel in our car for the next day and allowed us to stop by the local 99 cent store, which had milk, eggs, and a limited amount of produce, and pick up groceries. I know you may think this was horrible and extreme. But, I continued to restate to myself a statement Jerry Rice had made a few years back. Jerry Rice is considered to be one of the greatest wide receivers in NFL history and played for the San Francisco 49ers, the Oakland Raiders, and The Seattle Seahawks. He said, "I will do what others won't do, so I can do what others can't do." Through my commitment to make this happen, laser focused on the prize, things started turning around. Over the next 8 months a system was born.

In the first month, without any system, just massive activity in the marketplace walking into businesses, we earned $2,500. However, the process was too time consuming, the income wasn't consistent, and the rejection level was **HUGE!!!** If anyone tells you to "Go Walk Your Community" (code for go cold call on businesses) they probably have never done it or they wouldn't recommend it to you. If they have done it and they still recommend it, they don't care what level of rejection you're about to be exposed to. What I know is we couldn't generate consistent income doing it so we refined our methods, tested, and measured the results. Refined our methods again, tested further, and measured the results. We went to different trainings and picked up an idea here, a technique there, and refined our methods, tested and measured the results. I read books and picked up an idea here and a technique there, and refined our methods, tested, and measured the results. 8 Months later we were National Top Producers with a system in place.

At the next convention, we were recognized in two Biz Plan categories as National Top Producers, the Legal Plan for Self-Employed (now the Biz Plan 10) and the Business Owners Legal Solutions Plan (now the Biz Plan 50).

We were standing back stage with the other Top Producers, waiting to be called to get our awards. We had earned the #2 spot for the Legal Plan for the Self-Employed, and the associates who earned #1 and #3 spots were an up-line and his front-line associate. The up-line had earned the #1 spot and his down-line had earned the #3 spot. They had been doing real estate seminars of some kind together and at the end of the seminar they would offer the biz plan to agents in attendance. What was shocking to me was when the up-line associate, who earned the #1 spot shared with me how he got the #1 spot and his down-line ended up with the #3 spot. He shared that as the end of the year was coming he realized his recruit was ahead of him. So, he told him he could take a couple weeks off and he continued to put memberships in to pass up his down-line and secure the #1 spot. I thought this is wrong. He robbed his own front-line recruit of the award. This guy seemed to me to be so arrogant. He was completely okay with what he had done. What was more shocking to me was he was so comfortable with it that he was sharing this with me right in front of his down-line team member.

He then asked, "How long have you been marketing Biz Plans?" I said, "We started 8 months ago" and I couldn't resist so I continued, "So, if you're going to be #1 next year you're going to have to pick it up a little." Thinking back, I probably shouldn't have said that. But, the guy needed a little attitude adjustment. I never saw him again and he was never recognized again as a Top Producer.

That year the company ran a production contest where the winners would be featured in the "Success from Home" Magazine. We worked our butts off to earn that spot and a year after being recruited by a "Success from Home" magazine, we were featured in the magazine. The magazine was going to be released at convention and I couldn't wait to get there to buy some so I could see how it came out. What a difference a year can make.

We went on to accomplish Executive Director on personal production the end of that second year. At our ED celebration, the wife of my up-line Gold ED who had said we shouldn't market Biz Plan because it wasn't "CORE", wasn't the Traditional Teaching or system, came and congratulated us for making it happen. She said, "I didn't think you could do it, but you did."

CAUTION: When you venture outside of the "traditional" system, in a lot of cases your up-line will not be supportive. That is until they see the overrides start rolling in. Then the tune will change to "Go Boy, or Girl Go!"

Over the years we were privileged enough to earn corporate trips. It was the trip to Lake Tahoe where we first met Nick Serba.

Nick Serba is a Millionaire Club Member and was head of Biz Plan sales for Pre-Paid Legal at the time. Even at this early stage of our business, our Biz Plan production had been mentioned on the Small Biz conference call several times and when we saw Nick Serba, we went up to introduce ourselves. I'm know Nick meets people all the time. When we went up to him and introduced ourselves and shared we were marketing Biz Plans he said, "Great! I hope to hear your names on the Small Biz Call." I said we have been mentioned on the Small Biz call. He then asked for our business card. Within a few days, Jeff Cordle, who ran GoSmallBiz back then, gave us a call and asked if we would come on the call and be interviewed. We agreed and that began a long relationship with GoSmallBiz. Over the next several years we were invited to speak at numerous Boot Camps and teach before National Conventions.

On our second trip to Atlanta to speak at the GoSmallBiz Bootcamp, we were driving down the Interstate and got a call from a number I didn't recognize. So, I let it go to voice mail. When I listened to the message it was Nick Serba and he wanted to invite us to come up to his mountain home outside of Atlanta and spend the night if we had time. When I listened to the message I couldn't believe it. I thought my up-line or someone was playing a practical joke on us. But no, it was Nick Serba. Did we have the time? We made the time and that was the most amazing time in my life. What an honor it was to be able to hang out with and stay at a multimillionaire's home. It was amazing to be able to spend time with him and his wife Gale, an accomplished business woman and get to know them personally. It was a transformational experience for us.

Over the next several years we were asked to participate on countless Small Business conference calls where we shared tips on how other associates could achieve the same level of success we were having.

The second corporate trip we earned was to Huntington Beach. In addition to the trip, we had won a production contest where we earned dinner with Mr. Stonecipher.

Mr. Stonecipher couldn't make it so we had dinner with Mark Brown in his Presidential Suite, still an unbelievable experience.

The place was like a house with an entry way, living room, and dining room. It was pretty amazing. Mark was the Chief Marketing officer of Pre-Paid Legal at the time, a Millionaire Club Member, and later became the CO-CEO of Pre-Paid Legal with Randy Harp. The dinner was incredible and the conversation with Mark was amazing.

As our work marketing Biz Plans continued and we continued to share and teach what we were doing, we were invited to be featured in the "Small Business Report" magazine, based on our production and contributions to the Small Biz Division. We went on to receive numerous National Top Producer Awards, including the 1,000 Golden App Award.

I believe it was our third-year marketing Small Biz Plans when we were recognized and received our 1,000 Golden App Award. At that Convention, we were standing in line back stage to go out and receive our Award. As we were waiting, I was talking to the gentlemen who was standing in front of us. As it turns out, he had been in the business 11 years, and he was focused in group sales. He was being recognized at the same time for the same award we were getting after 3 years of marketing Biz Plans. He was a super nice guy and I was really happy for him as this is an incredible accomplishment for anyone in the business. However, at the same time I was thinking how fortunate we were for discovering the system I'll be sharing in this book which allowed us to accomplish the 1,000 Golden App Award in only 3 years. Only a year later we received our 2,000 Golden App Award.

To help more people accomplish greater success marketing Biz Plans, I created the Advanced Small Biz Training Program. This training has evolved over the years into what is the CORE Method Training and Support Program today. We've taken over 4,000 associates through the Advanced Small Biz Training Program (ASBT) since its inception, across this country at live events, before National Conventions and Boot Camps.

This training has been streamed LIVE over the internet and was made available as an On-Demand On-Line Training Program. I've written three books on marketing Biz Plan and making a 6-figure income which are available on Amazon, including this book you're reading now. Like other Top Producers have shared in their stories as their businesses evolved and grew, their lives changed, the cars we drove changed, as well as their zip code, so did ours.

More importantly it allowed me the time and income to be a real parent.

As I mentioned earlier, I had a successful Corporate America career which allowed me to earn a multiple six figure income. What it didn't offer though was an opportunity to be a parent and participate in my children's life at the level I wanted to. The company I managed operated 24 hours a day. I would leave my house before my kids got up so I could be at the office before the first shift finished. I would stay during the second shift and until the third shift had started to make sure everything was running smoothly. By the time I got home, my kids were already in bed. I would have some time on Saturday for family and then Sunday I had to go in and open the building so the equipment could be turned on, so it was warmed up and ready to begin work for first shift on Monday. Yes, I was making good money. Yes, I had a nice care and lived in a nice house. But those things are not what life is all about. Family is. Because of the system I'm going to share in this book we were able to do this business and not have to work jobs like most people are required to do. It allowed us to be the parents we always wanted to be.

I don't know about you, or if you can relate to this, but I loved watching my kids at their sports practices and compete.

One day after watching my son at his Varsity swim practice, he came up to me and said, "My coach came up to me today and asked why you were here all the time. He thinks he's in trouble or something when he sees you." My son said he told him, "He just likes watching me practice." I thought it both funny and sad so few parents can be at their kid's practices, the coach thought it odd when one showed up. But it didn't matter to me, I loved watching them and my business gave me this opportunity.

Our business allowed us to travel the country with our kids, allowing them to see things most people don't get to see in their entire life. Which was such a blessing.

But, it wasn't always easy. There was a lot of work which went into discovering the system which would work consistently. However, once I made the decision to work in the Small Biz Division, I committed to monthly certification training. Each month I would go to the class, take what I learned and apply it into the field. The next month I would go back and learn some more. Because I had been working in the field, each month I would hear the same information differently. It made more sense and I picked up new nuggets each month.

As my business grew I traveled across the country and took certification training with different instructors to get their unique prospective and tips. All valuable nuggets. However, while each certification trainer had some great information, each were missing key elements to make it work as a full-time income. Most were teaching theory backed by their own previous experience doing something else like group sales or a previous business background. We took what we learned and applied it to our activity, tested and tweaked it until we had a system that would produce consistent predictable results.

Once we hit ED on personal production, all the local ED's wanted us to come teach their team what we were doing. I decided if we were going to teach anyone, we would teach everyone, and the Advanced Small Biz Training Program was born. This training program was an independent program that I created and taught through my company, CORE Biz Systems.

Over the next several years, working in conjunction with GoSmallBiz, we would be asked to speak at GoSmallBiz Boot Camps, teach before National Conventions, and we traveled across the country teaching the Advanced Small Biz Training Program to local markets. From the income we earned through our personal Biz Plan sales production and training activities from my company, CORE Biz Systems, I discovered what I consider to be my calling in life, my passion, helping associates and direct sales reps accomplish more in their business. Helping them Break Free from Traditional Training and apply logical business and sales principles to their business so they can produce consistent predictable income. Running CORE Biz Systems and helping associates and direct sales reps is now my full-time focus. It is such a blessing to be able to make a difference in the lives of so many associates and direct sales reps working to make their businesses produce an income they can live on.

The training has evolved over the years and is now encompassed in my CORE Method Community. The CORE Method Community is an exclusive membership based training and coaching program which is available to Associates focused on marketing Biz Plans and SmallBiz Plans at a level beyond what Traditional Training Supports.

But this book isn't about me. It's about the system we discovered and how you can use it in your business right now to get similar results if you apply what I will be sharing in this book correctly and with a commitment to succeed. No hype, no palm palms. Just a simple step-by-step strategy for building a solid business and income.

The cool thing is it works for virtually anyone regardless of availability, experience level, or marketplace. It works if you're just starting out, or if you're a more seasoned associate. It works regardless of gender or ethnicity. But don't take my word for it. Here's what associates are saying about the CORE Method:

"This is a guide through the maze. It's been a maze all these years and I've been doing this a long time. And even though it can be a maze, this is like a guide that gets you from the beginning to the end, or what I like to call the prize. For me it has really opened a lot of doors and a lot of great understanding of how the process works. Because I've been through the leads, through everything trying to get businesses and this really makes sense to me"

- **Sandra, LegalShield Associate**

"If I can master the 9-Step program you have, at my age, I won't have to make all the mistakes of going through the school of hard knocks!"

- **George, LegalShield Associate**

OMG Charlie! It works just like you said!!! The day after your training I signed up a new Biz Plan Client and got 4 Biz Plan referrals.

- **Joan, LegalShield Associate**

As a member of the Core Method Training and Support Group, I'm learning a lot about building my business with a focus on servicing Small Business owners. Charlie has provided clear, step by step guidelines to move my business from where I am to where I want to be. His training makes it plain, gives clear directions and practical application on how to get from point A to point B. The support group provides encouragement, recognition and some regular accountability as we move through the nine steps. I really appreciate Charlie's coaching because I feel he really cares about each of us as a person as well as seeing us succeed as business owners.

- **Vernessa, LegalShield Associate**

This is just a few examples of the emails I get from associates. The bottom line is, this has worked across the country to help associates increase their production, their income, and consistently qualify for Performance Club.

So, think about this for just a minute...

What if you could eliminate all the stress and frustration of struggling to make a consistent income from your business and start making sales right away?

What would it mean for your business, your life, and your family to finally have a step-by-step system where you could get predictable results? No more hope marketing.

What if you could 2x, 5x, or even 10x your leads and customers in your business? Clients on demand!

What if you could Break Free?

Does that sound cool to you?

Okay I thought so, let's get growing!

Let's cover the objectives I have and the three game changing secrets I have in this book:

1) How to identify your ideal client prospect to increase your results and set you up to be able to quickly scale your business.
2) How you can build momentum in your business so you can scale your business and generate consistent income.
3) How you can win at this and quickly scale your business and your income so you can generate a consistent, predictable income.

These are my objectives for you so you can launch a successful strategy for getting in front of business owners right away and go from zero to consistent income quicker and easier than you could using the Traditional Methods and Training while cutting out 90% of the time and guess work.

Does that sound cool?

Perfect!

Let's begin.

THE SYSTEM

If you're like most associates, you're suffering from what I call B2B Frustrations. You're in a total state of training overwhelm and method confusion trying to figure out what tool to use, whose advice to follow, what to say, and who to say it to.

You're likely suffering from information overload. Yuck! That's where you're consuming conference calls, on-line training videos, going to training events, breakout sessions...drinking from a fire hose. Just a ton of content and nothing makes sense or fits together in one coherent strategy and it's not working for you in the real world.

You might even be spending tons of time and money and still not have an effective strategy in place for making consistent income from your business.

I completely understand where you're at. I was there also. Attending weekly briefings, the meetings after the meetings, Super Saturdays, Monday conference calls which went one after another, team conference calls, B2B conference calls. It was endless and the flow of information, most conflicting with the next was overwhelming.

To combat all this in the beginning, I focused on the calls and training events which were intended for my area of focus, marketing Biz Plans. As I mentioned, as soon as I made the decision to get different results and focus on Biz Plan marketing I went to Small Biz Certification Training every month. The trainer was awesome, always willing to take time to talk to me about my specific circumstances and he had a lot of previous business experience. The problem was the marketing method he was teaching was not something he had actually tested with my specific need for production. He was teaching theory of what had worked for him under difference circumstances and he thought might work for us also. Thankfully with his theory, our brainstorming, consulting with my up-line Gold ED, doing a ton of reading, a lot of testing and analyzing the results which came from it, I was ultimately able to create the CORE Method and provide you with the information in this book.

However, while I was trying to figure all this out, I would get on every Small Biz Conference call and listen to all the people they had on the call who were supposedly getting all these fantastic results. The problem was they weren't. When I looked up their names on the leader board, they either weren't there, or weren't producing consistent sales. They were getting sporadic results at best. After listening to them and comparing what I was experiencing in the field, I knew what they were sharing was either untested theory or an isolated, sporadic, random result I couldn't reproduce, and not something I should try myself. They should have included that disclaimer you see on the extreme sports broadcasts, "Please Don't Try This at Home", at the beginning of the call.

If you've been trying to market Biz plans, have been trying to implement what you've learned from the Traditional Training or from what you hear on conference calls and aren't getting the results you hoped for, don't be too hard on yourself. Here's the good news and I wish I would have learned this from the beginning, it's not your fault.

You see everyone else has a clear path to success. Think about it. Doctors, Lawyers, Suba Divers, Short Order Cooks, Policewomen and men, Fire Fighters, Pilots, Nurses, Navy Seals, you name it. You show up, you go through training that gives you everything you need to know…leaving nothing out. You get certified, you get on the job training, you work your job, and you achieve your goal. There is a clear path from point A to point B for everyone except you, the Independent B2B Associate. There's no clear path to success being taught. There's no step-by-step path from point A to point B. The Traditional Training doesn't provide it and neither does the information you hear on conference calls.

One of the reasons you might be struggling is what I call, "the G Myth." That's where all the "GURUs", leaders, even trainers, are pushing small pieces of the puzzle, but you're missing key ingredients required for success. I'm sure they don't mean any harm by it. But missing these key ingredients is devastating to your income, time, and pocketbook while you waste tons of time and money trying to figure it all out. They want to get you to this event, or that training, and you end up getting nickel and dimed you to death.

They're also pushing cookie cutter strategies that aren't tailored to your exact circumstances, availability, and marketplace. So, the traditional training says, here's how you get business owners to luncheons. Here's how you talk to people you do business with. Here's how you "Go Walk Your Community" (which is code for Cold Calling). But it doesn't make sense for your exact experience level, comfort level, or circumstances, and these strategies are incomplete and puts the sales process out of order and out of your control.

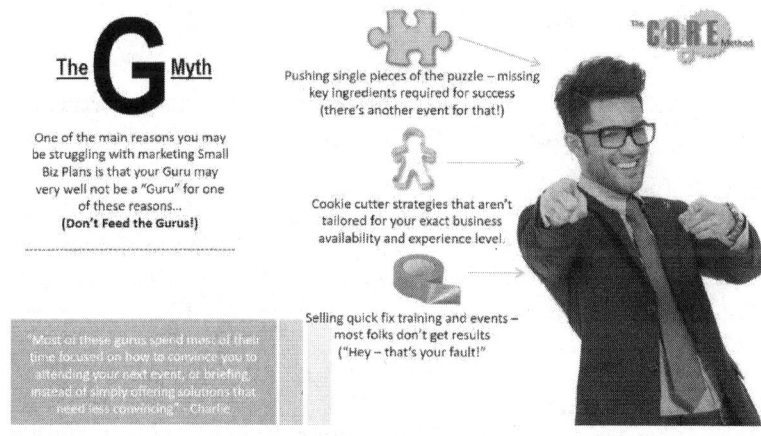

They also sell quick fixes and tools which are supposed to do everything for you, like on-line sales videos and auto responder systems. Lots of associates fail to get the results they're looking for using these tools and methods.

Then when it doesn't work they say, hey you didn't implement it correctly, or you didn't give it enough time and effort so it's your fault. There's a lot of nonsense floating around out there that we're going to cut through starting right now.

So, let's zoom out and see the forest from the trees, or the planets from the stars, and let me share a clear, step-by-step path to success marketing Biz Plans and SmallBiz Plans.

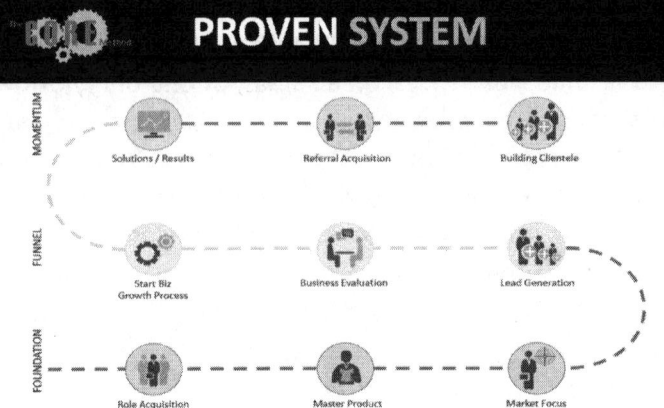

This system applies to all three types of associates, spare-time, part-time, and full-time. This system applies regardless of your experience level, whether you're just starting out or whether you're a more season associate as it starts from scratch and builds your knowledge with each step, so you can use this system to start or scale your business. This system works regardless of your marketplace as it can be customized to your specific market, and it works regardless of your gender or ethnicity because of the unique way in which you position yourself and approach the marketplace.

In this book, I will cover the three core steps of this system so you can get started right away. But, first I need you to go on a strict information diet. What's a "Strict Information Diet?" I need to you to eliminate all the other conflicting voices you're plugged in to allow you to get the most out of this book and be able to effectively implement what I will be sharing. For you this might be conference calls, up-line and sideline input, Gurus, even training which isn't giving you the information you need to accomplish your goals.

You see, to get the results you're looking for you will need to implement this system step-by-step. To do this you must eliminate all the noise that may distract you or cause you to question which path you should take. Always remember, a double minded man is weak in all areas, or one of my favorites lines is from the movie "Sweet Home Alabama" when the character Melanie Smooter, played by Reese Witherspoon, is talking to her dad about whether to re-unite with her husband or marry her fiancé. Her dad gave her some great advice when he famously said, "you can't ride two horses with one ass, Sugar Plum." This is what most associates try to do. They plug into everything and the flow of conflicting information is so great they never accomplish anything because of the confusion, overwhelm, and missing pieces to the puzzle.

If you agree to go on a strict information diet, I am going to give you a very powerful system and tools you can use to get started right away.

Remember when I said there was a moment when everything changed, when the system was born? You see my past 30 years of experience was running businesses. When you're running a business, you must have systems and frameworks in place so everyone knows what they're supposed to be doing to get a specific outcome.

Businesses don't do random. At least not the ones that succeed. Boeing for example sets their sights 10 years ahead and then creates a plan to get there. Everything they do is planned and orchestrated to bring that vision into reality. You could imagine without a clear vision and systems and frameworks in place, nothing would progress in an organized manner, profits would disappear, and Boeing would be out of business. They must be able to invest money and get a return on that investment to stay in business, they must make profits. The only way to do this is with systems and frameworks.

Many years later when I was trying to figure out how to get predictable results marketing Biz Plans, we put systems and frameworks in place so we could plan and duplicate activities, track progress, and measure results. By doing this, we could see exactly where adjustments needed to be made to bring our production and income to the level we wanted. It also allowed us to duplicate by being able to share this method with others.

Once we put the system in place, everything changed. We were able to get a consistent, predictable outcome that we could track and measure. You can cut out 90% of the frustration and pain by working within a system. So, as I walk you through this system, I'm going to show you frameworks for literally every step, you're going to get access to a one-page marketing strategy, and I'm going to show you how you can use frameworks to kind of short cut your progress and really get the job done quickly.

THE FOUNDAITON

The first part I'm going to cover is the Foundation.

In the Traditional Training, everyone wants to talk about tools and approaches, but the truth is if you nail the foundation everything else becomes fill in the blank.

Think of it like an iceberg that has 20% of its mass floating above the water. That 20% is what you've probably learned from Traditional Training. It is the activities you're encouraged to do. Make a list, follow your dollar, go walk your community...all these activities you've been taught are just the top 20% of the iceberg. Without the other 80% you're dead in the water, and your sub is sunk. Most associates try to operate their business with just that 20% taught at the Traditional Training. But as I said, that 20% is missing key elements required for success.

Within the foundation is:

1. Role Acquisition - The role you must play in your business to accomplish success
2. Product Mastery – Mastering the Products on a practical application level

3. Market focus – Understanding who your ideal client prospects are and why this specific target is so vital to your success.

These three elements are responsible for 80% of your success. Your entire business should be built on these three key elements. But while the Traditional Training teaches smooth catch phrases, massive activity, and lots of excitement (the octopus on roller skates approach), most of your success lies beneath the surface with the foundation, these three key elements which will dictate everything else you do in your business. What I've discovered from my own business and working with associates who I've taken through the CORE Method as part of my CORE Method Training and Support Program, if you get the foundation right the rest falls into place.

Nailing the foundation sets you apart from everyone else and is how you go from totally invisible in your marketplace, hunting for each new sale, humiliating yourself, and begging business owners to sit down with you. Too completely irresistible where business owners look at you as an equal, want to sit down with you, and want your help to grow and protect their business. It's that powerful and it's almost fail safe because you've done the homework and taken the time to lay your solid foundation you can build massive success on.

More importantly, Its super simple!

So, let's dive in.

ROLE ACQUISITION

The first part of the foundation is having the right mindset and assuming the role of a business owner in your business rather than an employee. Simply put, having a business owner's mindset.

Understand in the training I give our members of the CORE Method Training and Support Program, I go through all the roles an associate should play in their business. But I'm going to buzz through them so you can get to the most important one.

As a B2B Associate you must assume the role of a business owner. This is far more critical when you're focused on B2B Sales because there isn't a lot of up-line support. Their lack of support is not because they don't care about your success, or because you've ventured out of the traditional recruiting system. In most cases they would love to support you and help you, they just don't know how. When you are working in the recruiting system, having this mindset is less important because you have your up-line with some experience in this area. They will encourage you to attend the events which will support your recruiting efforts. They will encourage the activities you should be engaged in. In some cases, they can even help you with presentations and trouble shooting. However, when you're focused on B2B sales, in most cases, you are left to your own demise. You must be self-motivated, be able to track and analyze your business, do your own presentations, track your profits, and be committed to hitting your goals. Basically, you're operating without a safety net and direct support so you must have the mindset the buck stops here, and if it's meant to be it's up to me. The mindset of a business owner.

The other HUGE benefit to having this entrepreneurial business owner mindset is it allows you to transition from an employee to a business owner. It allows you to focus on what Jim Rohn taught through his life, profits are better than wages.

As a business owner, you take responsibility for the results your business is getting, and you're always working to make the most money you can in the time allowed...always focused on results and profits. To do this you must be a marketer, a sales person, accountant, and a supervisor for your business. Being self-employed means, you employ yourself to run your business. To do this you must always try to work as efficiently as possible to make as much profits as possible.

SUCCESS VS FAILURE

Associate/Business Owner	VS	Employee
• Define their own goals		• Relies on someone else to define their goals
• Define their own responsibilities		• Relies on someone else to define their responsibilities
• Define your own priorities		• Relies on, or allows someone else to set or change their daily priorities (family and friends)
• Define their own daily activities		• Relies on someone else to define their daily activities
• Determines their success and progress		• Relies on someone else to determine progress
• Does as much as possible to make a much profit as possible		• Do as little as possible to make the agreed upon income
• You Manage Your Time to accomplish your goals		• Relies on, or allows someone else to manage their time, OR use up their time.

A business owner sets goals and works within systems and frameworks to accomplish them. Operating your Biz Plan marketing efforts with this mindset is critical to your success. Without assuming this role and having this mindset nothing else I'm going to share in this book will matter.

Early on in my business I was out in the field with an associate and I was trying to convey this mindset to her. She was struggling to achieve consistent income and activity in her business and thus unable to get consistent results. I was trying to explain to her how important it is to have a business owner's mindset and operate her business like a business. Have specific business hours, be focused on your business activities when engaged in them, and always be working to be profitable. What she said in response shined a light on her challenges and helped her discover the self-created obstacle which was blocking her. She said, "Well,

Charlie, this isn't a real business." I must have looked like a deer in the headlights when she said it. But, her flawed philosophy about her business was the root of her challenges. Even though she had joined the business and wanted to earn money she wasn't looking at her business as a business...like the businesses she was trying to help. She was looking at her business as something less than a business, almost like a hobby. She had overhead expenses, a phone bill, had to keep the lights on at her home office, had to make a business vehicle payment, had to maintain insurance on that vehicle, and had to meet payroll to be able to pay herself. To do that she had to earn a profit. She had to think like a business owner.

Once she realized this, and I mean on a foundational level, her business changed. She allocated the time to do her business, she approached business owners differently. She started adding new clients on a consistent basis. Her mindset had shifted to taking responsibility for her business and making sure her business was earning profits. To work for results, not just doing activity and going through the motions.

Always maintain the mindset of a business owner in everything you do in your business. It will guide you to the things you need to do and when you need to do them, focused on results, and show you the things you need to avoid.

PRODUCT MASTERY

The next part of the foundation is product mastery.

Most associates don't take the time to learn the practical application of their core products, the Biz Plans with the GoSmallBiz add-on and the SmallBiz Plans. Consequently, when they sit down with a business owner they don't know how to share the information effectively to provide the solutions which will help the business owner grow and protect their business.

Armed with a tool, some cute catch phrases they might hear on a conference call, training, or event, and a focus on fear marketing (sharing all the horrible things that might happen if they don't get the service) the average associate fails miserably at marketing biz plans. Once this failure occurs the average associate shifts their focus to either trying to recruit the business owner away from their business and into LegalShield, or they sell them a family plan and call it a day. When they do this, they leave two or three hundred dollars sitting on the table (their profits), fail to properly protect the business owner and provide them with the solutions they truly need to effectively operate and grow their business. They also megaphone the MLM mantra and connect LegalShield and all other associates to Network Marketing in the business owner's mind.

Most associates follow the Traditional Training which is to get tools into the marketplace. Doing this puts the sales process out of order and out of your control as you share features and benefits instead of solutions before you determine the need. Remember my Submarine analogy? Moving the prospect forward through a logical progression to get the results you're looking for, a new client. This can't happen when you get the sales process out of order and lose control of the process. You end up chasing prospects and wasting time which chews up your profits.

The Traditional Training implements what is known in marketing terms as "hope Marketing" by sharing a tool, getting a prospect into the autoresponder, or sharing a canned corporate presentation HOPING the business owner will see some feature or benefit they can use or sees value in. What they don't realize is features and benefits don't sell, solutions do. They're **hoping** to make sales and recruit people without putting an effective marketing strategy in place. **Remember,** Business Owner, Mindset. Using Hope Marketing and trying to let tools and technology do the work for you will only reduce closing ratios, limit your success, and cause you to struggle to make a profit. These Traditional Methods requires the business owner to connect the dots and realize all the practical applications of the biz plan from the features and benefits you've shared. The truth is most won't make the connection. Even if they have a need, by the time all the features and benefits of the biz plan have been shared, you've talked the business owner out of buying because the list of things they don't need far outweighs the list of things they need.

As I was going through the newly released SmallBiz Certification training and watching the Flip Chart presentation I was shocked at how little the business owner talked verses how much the Associate who was doing the presentation. A perfect example of sharing features and benefits. You should also notice during that example the presentation started before the associate determined what the business owner needed, so she was just sharing features and benefits trying to find something the business owner would connect with.

Imagine stopping by a car dealership and as soon as you get out of the car the salesperson, without determining why you're there, puts you in the dealership shuttle and starts driving you around the lot showing you cars. He takes you from one car to the next explaining how awesome the car is, all the features and benefits, the safety awards they have received and so on. After an hour of this he pulls you into the showroom and says, okay let's fill out the contracts. Can you imagine! The salesperson had no idea what you needed in a car, which car you were interested in, or if you wandered onto the lot to get directions or use the restroom. This is what is going on when you follow the Traditional Training.

People don't buy features and benefits, they buy solutions. It's been my experience if you follow the Traditional Training as presented, your closing ratios will be very low. As a business owner is sitting listening to your spiel, if they connect the dots at all, they're making two lists in their mind. The first list is things they might need. The second list is things they don't need. When the list of things they don't need gets bigger than the things they might need you've lost the sale, and your sub is sunk.

The other problem with getting tools in the marketplace is you lose control of the presentation. You get the cart before the horse and the business owner pre-judges if they want to sit down with you or purchase your stuff. Think of it like a card game. The cards go down at the proper time, in the proper order, never at the start of the game, or even before it begins. Like the submarine analogy I shared at the beginning of this book, you need to work within a system moving the prospect from compartment to compartment in the proper order. This allows you to maintain control over the sales experience and *guide* the business owner to the desired conclusion. Get things out of order and like I said, your sub is sunk.

So why does the Traditional Training teach this approach? Because the average associate can get tools into the marketplace. Remember how I got recruited from a magazine left in a Doctor's office? I had a need and connected the dots. However, this is not an effective use of your tools or your money. Can you imagine how many people came in contact with that magazine before I did? Perhaps 50 or 60 people a day for however many days it was sitting there. While hundreds of associates put magazines in the marketplace few get recruited from them. However, it is a simple activity which can be taught to the masses to get those average associates doing something. Through this massive activity by hundreds or thousands of associates enough sales are made to keep the company profitable and moving forward. However, the average associate can't survive on the income from this Traditional Method of marketing, and neither can you. You must do things different from the average associate if you expect above average results from your business. Thus, the CORE Method.

MAKE A NOTE of this one tip. It can help you make thousands of dollars: *Features and Benefits don't sell, solutions do.*

Think about it, when was the last time you bought something based on the features and benefits? Probably never. You bought based on a solution the product or service was going to provide for you. Features and benefits probably didn't play big a role in the purchase.

The last time you purchased a car did you purchase it based on a feature or benefit? Probably not, you purchased it based on a specific need you had and the car you purchased provided a solution to that need. You needed to go fast, or slow. You needed a car to carry your kids and all their gear, or all your grandkids and their gear. You might have purchased it because it fit in a specific price range you needed to stay within. But the primary reason for the purchase was to solve a need you had.

The same is true when marketing Biz Plans, and I will go into greater details later. The point is without spending the time to learn the practical application of the Biz Plans with GoSmallBiz add-on or the SmallBiz Plans, you can't share a solution when a need is presented to you. **Take the time to discover what the plan does, how it does it, and understand under what circumstances it's specific benefit would be utilized.** This is where the money is made. Every challenge a business owner faces can be helped through either the law firm or the consultants at GoSmallBiz...*Every Challenge!* You're a problem solver. It's your job to ask the right questions, be a good listener, and help the business owner with solutions through the Biz Plans. Throwing up a canned LegalShield commercial as to why the business owner needs what you have to offer, in my experience, is not an effective approach.

Business owners purchase things they need, and they purchase based on belief. Your practical product knowledge needs to be at a level where you can transfer your true belief you can help them, so they can have the same belief. A business owner will never have greater belief in the product than you do. Understanding the membership at a practical application level will allow you to share a solution the Biz Plan with GoSmallBiz add-on or the SmallBiz Plan can provide the prospect to overcome their challenges or reach their goals with conviction. To get this level of understanding look at each benefit and make

70 | P a g e

sure you clearly understand under what situations each benefit can be utilized. What problems or challenges does it help solve. As you're sitting with a business owner and talking with them, listen for challenges the business owner is experiencing or goals they are trying to achieve. Think of what specific benefits would help them to overcome those challenges or help them achieve their goals faster and cheaper than they could on their own. Being able to explain with conviction how those challenges could be overcome, or goals can be reached, by using the Biz Plan and GoSmallBiz add-on or the SmallBIz to obtain solutions is the level of practical knowledge you must have.

Make a Note: *The Business Owner is not buying the membership based on their belief in the company or service, they're buying based on their belief in what you're saying it can do. You must transfer your true belief when sharing the solution and to do that you must know the product at a practical application level.*

MARKET FOCUS

The third part of your foundation is your market focus. Getting this right will determine whether you'll be able to reach consistent income and momentum, or struggle for your next sale.

Often when I ask an associate, who is your ideal client prospect? I will get the answer, "everyone is my ideal client." The truth is, while everyone may be able to purchase one of the plans you offer, everyone is not your ideal client prospect.

Renowned Marketer, Copy Writer, and Author of the "No BS" series of business how to books, Dan Kennedy, shared a profound statement at a marketing conference I attended in St Louis a few years ago. He said, "If your marketing and sales efforts are for everyone, they're for no one." What he meant by this was there is no way you can create a marketing and sales strategy that can possibly encompass everyone. If you were to attempt to do this your focus will be so broad your message or approach wouldn't connect with anyone. However, this blanket, shotgun approach is what the Traditional Training teaches and the average associate follows. Missing this key element is one of the main reasons most don't make money at this. To make real money marketing Biz Plans and be able to generate consistent income, you must be very focused on **WHO** you're going to spend your time pursuing so you can make the *greatest profits*, always thinking like a business owner. Here is a fact you would be well served to remember: Some businesses will help you make money and scale your business, and some will cost you money and prevent grow.

You need to know which is which and where to focus your attention.

With LegalShield so focused on group business, most associates are chasing what I refer to as the elephant. In my live training events I always ask, how many of you have seen an elephant in the wild? Typically, no one raises their hands. Sure, we've seen them at the zoo, or perhaps at a circus, but roaming in the wild? Probably not unless you've been to Africa on a safari. I then ask, how many of you have seen a rabbit in the wild? And almost everyone raises their hand. Rabbits are EVERYWHERE!!! The moral to this story is if you want to starve to death, hunt elephants, at least in this country. But, if you want to keep yourself fed on a consistent basis, hunt rabbits.

I see group sales as the elephants, and while you may find one here and there, rabbits or Small Businesses who can use the Biz Plans are everywhere. They can be added to your client base more frequently and consistently **IF** you're using the right system.

When you bring on a new Biz Plan 50 with the GoSmallBiz add-on Client, you earn about $375 in upfront commissions as a Director. When you bring on a new SmallBiz Pro Client, you earn about $400 in upfront commissions. But what this new client should be able to do, if it's the right business, is lead you to other Small Business Owners they know and you can work with through referrals. If your average new client gives you just 6 referrals and you can add 50% of those referrals as new clients with the same membership, your numbers should be about 70-80% on referrals but let's say just 50%, you would earn an additional $1,138 - $1194. This brings your total commissions earned, originating from that initial business to between $1,518 and $1,592. Not bad, huh?

Now if you still want to pick up some group business, those businesses you've added as clients can refer you to other larger companies you can open groups in. The difference is, you will be going to those businesses from a referral which will give you quicker access and instant credibility based on the business who referred you.

If you open a group in a business referred to you by your four new Biz Plan clients with twenty employees signing up, you would earn somewhere around $1,600 or more as a Director, in up front commissions. That would bring your total commissions originating from your initial Biz Plan Client to between $3,118 - $3,192. Now that's not bad, is it?

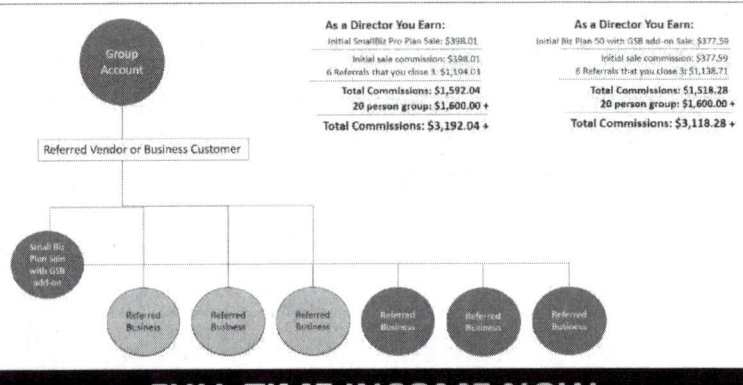

FULL-TIME INCOME NOW

So, who would your ideal target be who can deliver referrals to you on a consistent basis? Do some strategic planning and decode businesses in your marketplace to see who within your market is your best target and the best use of your time.

When you look at any business, you want to think about the need they have for the service. Remember, *features and benefits don't sell.* However, solutions do. You want to think about what need would any business you're looking at as a potential prospect have for the service. If you can't determine a need, skip that business. You want to work with business owners with the greatest need for multiple benefits, so you have the best chance of success. Now just because you can think of a list of possible needs doesn't mean the specific business owner you're going to be talking to will have those need. But what it does is give you a better chance at success. For example; if you have two businesses and you can

[Margin notes: SOLUTION SELL. NOT FEATURES OR BENEFITS.]

only think of a single need for one business; but the other business you can think of six potential needs for six different benefits. You would want to go to the one with the six potential needs, so you stack the deck in your favor giving you more chances to connect with a challenge they might have.

You also want to look for the potential the business has to lead you to another business through referrals. If you're looking at two businesses and one is a retail business, their customers are retail end user customers. It's extremely unlikely this business will give you access to their customer base. Now that business is doing business with other businesses through the vendors they use, so the potential for referrals still exists. However, you need to know where to look for them with each potential business you will be calling on. In addition to looking at who they purchase from, you should also look at who they sell to. Are they're customers other businesses? When you find a business who vendors are other businesses and they sell to other businesses, you have a much higher probability of getting referrals.

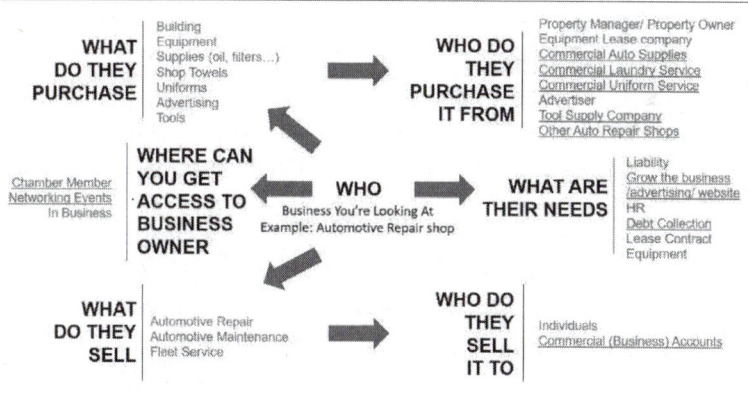

The point is, go where you are going to have the best chance of getting access to other businesses through referrals. Look at who they sell to and who they purchase goods and services from to determine if the prospective business you're looking at will likely be able to lead you to other businesses.

So, why is this key element so important? Because you need to be earning profits. Each new client you bring on costs money to acquire and to service after the sale. It may have taken one visit, or five or six visits to get them started as your new client. But each visit costs money. On the back end of the sale, after you have your new client, you must service the account for at least twelve months to make sure they stay on the books and don't cancel out causing you a charge back. Each visit to follow up with this client costs money. When you take your commission of let's say $400 and divide it by at least 12 visits, how much are you really making? About $33 before travel expenses, business expenses, and your time.

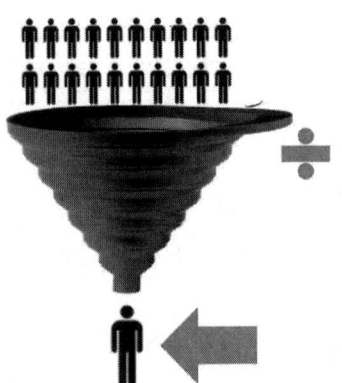

10 hours per week
x   4 weeks
40 hours to make sale
$377.59 Biz Plan 50 with GSB add-on
$9.44 Per Hour Before Expenses
$9.44 Fuel Costs
$9.44 Wear and Tear on you vehicle
$9.44 Vehicle Maintenance
$9.44 Cell Phone
$9.44 Clothing
$9.44 Tools
$9.44 Cost for meetings and events

Let me put it a different way. Let's say you spend 40 hours contacting twenty or so prospects to bring a new client on, get them started, and service their account. In the first twelve months, you're earning around $10.00 per hour. Just above minimum wage and that's before you pay your expenses. The only way this can change and you increase your income is if when you visit your client you're able to get referrals which will lead you to another $400 sale. Then you are earning money each time you follow up with your clients instead of costing money. But let's be clear, the only way you can get referrals is if your client has them to give. That's why some businesses will cost you money and some will help you to scale your business and make more money. Because whether your client is willing and able to give you referrals or not, you must still follow up with them and make sure they stay on the books. You must be okay with passing on the businesses that will cost you money, not provide referrals, and instead focus specifically on the ones who will help you to make money and scale your business by giving you referrals. This is the only way to scale your business and make consistent income marketing Biz Plans. **Please highlight and underline the last sentence so you remember it.**

Let me share the story of an associate I was coaching, I'm going to refer to him as Steve. Steve was struggling to generate consistent income from Biz Plan sales. It wasn't that he wasn't investing the time, money, and effort, he was. However, as he brought on new clients he couldn't get referrals. Because of this, after each new sale, he had to go back to the prospecting method he was using to get his last sale to generate his next sale. This cost him both time and money. Because of the length of time it took to generate the next sale using his prospecting method he was struggling to work his business as his primary income based on the little money he was earning. He became very frustrated because he wasn't making any headway to scale his business or get the consistency and income he was looking for. After looking over his clients it was obvious he wasn't focused on the right ideal target prospect so this was causing the challenge he was experiencing of not being able to get referrals. Market focus, looking for the right client is critical to scaling your business and making consistent income.

The last thing you want to look at is where can you get access to the prospective business? I am asked all the time how to get past a gatekeeper. I'm also asked what to do when you stop by a business which would be a great business prospect but the business owner is either never there or is never available. How do I overcome this? You don't. You move on to a business you can sit down with the business owner right off the bat and quit wasting your time. Don't let your ego get in the way of your profits. This is not a test of will, it is a test of efficiency and profitability. Wasting your time trying to sit down with someone who has either erected a wall by putting a gate keeper in place, or won't take the time to sit down with you is a no-win scenario. You will lose money on this prospect every time. Back to the numbers I shared above. You only make so much money per new client. If you spend all the commissions you earn chasing prospects you're not able to sit down with, for whatever reason, you have lost money. Multiply this over time and you're out of business, or spending more money than you're making to get the sale. Either way, that's not the vision. You must focus on businesses you are able to sit down with the business owner. Even if all the other elements are present except this one, you must skip the business and go where you have access to the business owner.

It is vitally important to your success, when you're looking at your prospective business owner, determine if you would have access to the business owner, where that access can occur, and the best time to accomplish that access as part of your market research.

I strongly encourage you to combine all these elements into a customer profile to determine exactly what businesses are you going to focus on. Once you have that client profile, or avatar as we call it in marketing, you base all your activities on whether that activity will put you in contact with that avatar or not. This will significantly increase your effectiveness when prospecting.

When you look at the Traditional Training which teaches "Go Walk Your Community", you're being taught to go door-to-door.

The challenge is you don't know who is on the other side. If they will be able to lead you to someone else, or even if you're likely to be able to see a business owner. The challenges go on and on which is why the rejection rate is so huge using this method. The ending result is the average associate quits after a few days of getting beat up. Through massive activity the Traditional Training teaches success will occur. However, common sense and a focus on profitability will eliminate this marketing approach from your arsenal.

Not focusing on the right targets will chew up your time, cost you money, lower your profits, and ultimately lead to your failure marketing biz plans. On the other hand, targeting the correct business to help you accomplish your goals of profitability and scalability will allow you to focus your marketing efforts and allow for success.

As you can see this is a clear path, a logical progression to help you get started making money on a consistent basis marketing Biz Plans and SmallBiz Plans. These three key elements; Assuming the Role of a Business Owner, Product Mastery at a Practical Application Level, and Accurate Market Focus will help you to build a solid business foundation

THE SALES FUNNEL

The next step in the CORE Method is the sales funnel. A sales funnel, simply put, is the activities you do to move a prospect through the sales process. Done correctly it will take you from a trickle of leads to a flood of prospect. The power of clients on demand.

There are three elements of the sales funnel

1. Leads Generation
2. Business Evaluation of your prospect's business
3. Getting the prospect started with one of the Biz Plans

If done correctly a business owner will move through this process with you and come to their own conclusion they need the service. This process is a conversation with the business owner, not an interrogation or hard sell. Always keep in mind, Features and Benefits don't sell, Solutions do. In order to provide solutions you must first understand the needs.

LEADS GENERATION

The first part of the sales funnel is leads generation. Creating the ultimate leads magnet where people want to talk and meet with you. Yes, there's a system and a framework for lead generation. Always remember, no one wants to be sold (features and benefits). But everyone wants to buy (solutions). Any method which asks a business owner to sit down with you so you can show them what you have to offer is a sales approach or a request to sell the business owner something. Using these approaches will significantly reduce your ability to get appointments because the business owner doesn't want to be sold.

The first part of lead generation is determining what your lead magnet will be. What would get a business owner to **want** to sit down with you? Your introduction along with a request for an appointment to discuss something which is mutually beneficial should be solid. For example; setting an appointment to see how you might be able to work with each other and refer business to each other. This would help expand their business and in return they might be able to help you expand yours. Nothing is being sold here and most business owners will be more open to cooperating to expand business than they will be to sit down with you to hear your sales pitch.

NOTE: Do all things on purpose.

Do all things on purpose. In other words, each step in this system is specifically designed to move the prospect closer to becoming your new client. It's designed that way on purpose, up front, before a prospect is ever contacted. This way all the steps can be practiced and mastered. Think about a submarine. Each member of the crew is trained before they ever step foot on a sub. They know what their responsibilities will be and what activities they will perform ahead of time to get a desired outcome. Once on the sub they practice more until they can perform their duties with mastery and they continue to practice maintaining that level of mastery. Each compartment on a sub is specifically designed to perform a function to help the sub operate as effectively and efficiently as possible. It's amazing how many associates don't work out what they are going to say upfront. Consequently, they don't demonstrate confidence and can't establish the rapport and belief required to move a business owner to the next compartment, or step. Your elevator speech, method for developing rapport, and your method for setting an appointment with a business owner should be scripted, practiced until it is natural for you to say, polished, and automatic. Otherwise you come across unsure and questionable to the business owner. As Fran Tarkenton has said, people do business with people they know, like, and trust. Business Owners are getting an impression of you and making a judgment the first time you meet. Make sure you are prepared to have a competent and confident conversation with a business owner, and request an appointment without fumbling over your words. This will speak volumes to how the business owner perceives you.

Next, you should select a prospecting venue where you're going to be able to meet your ideal client prospects. Selecting a venue where your ideal prospect will be, and not just attending random venues, will increase your profits and reduce your time between sales. These venues should be selected based on your specific circumstances, available time, and the money you're able to invest. Networking events are a great choice and most marketplaces have a wide variety to choose from.

LEAD GENERATION

Cold Calling | Networking Events | Industry Expos | Business Seminars | Business Support Groups | Social Events | Business Contacts and Clients

Select events where you will be able to meet the specific business owners you've selected as your ideal clients. Don't waste your time at events where these business owners either aren't present or aren't a member.

I was sitting down with an associate who was using networking events as her prospecting venue. Each week she would drive a half hour to her event, spend about an hour at the event, and then travel the half hour home. She had been doing this for a year. I asked her how many new clients she had been able to bring on over the past year. She said five. So, a sale every other month or so. Certainly not enough to live off. Even though she has consistently participated in a networking event, the ideal clients she needed weren't members or participants. Her investment of time and money was not as effective as it could have been had she joined events where an ideal client who could lead her to other clients was a member.

Selecting the right networking group is as important as selecting the right ideal client prospect. Take the time to select carefully, looking at who participates in their meetings, who are the members of the networking group or event, and who may not participate in the meetings, but who you can access through the group and group directory.

FIND YOUR IDEAL PROSPECTS

Once you have the right venue where your ideal client prospects are participating, join the events and look for those specific ideal client prospects. Work the room, introduce yourself, and ask them what they do. Once you find your ideal client prospect utilize your script to set an appointment at their business.

You might ask when would be a good time to stop by their business to learn more about their business, and who would be an ideal client prospect for their business. You might also share you would like to share what you do, and see if you might be able to refer business back and forth with each other.

Networking is what these venues are for and when you follow this approach, it will be a pleasant surprise to the business owner. You will differ from the typical associate using the Traditional Training approach to set appointment to show them what you have to offer. This will allow you to build valuable working relationships as an equal rather than a salesperson

BUSINESS EVALUATION

The next part in the Sales Funnel is the business evaluation or business interview. Remember business owners buy what they need. **Highlight and underline the previous sentence so you remember it.** Business owners buy solutions to help them with either accomplishing the goals they have or to overcome the challenges they face. The most effective way to get a new client and help them grow and protect their business is to discover what they want to accomplish and what's holding them back from accomplishing it. Their goals and challenges.

If you follow the advice I gave you in the previous chapter to set an appointment, your appointment strategy will be to learn more about what they do and who their ideal client is, share what you do, and maybe work together to refer business. This is what we call in sales and marketing, Your Upfront Contract. It's an upfront agreement you have with the business owner about what your next meeting or conversation will be, the agenda. Take a few minutes to get to know the business owner and build rapport. Once you've taken a few minutes to allow everyone to be comfortable, restate your Upfront Contract. An example might be: (First Name of business owner), when we talked at (name of the event) we agreed to meet today to get a better understanding of what each of us do, who an ideal prospect would be for each other so we might be able to refer business back and forth. So, let me ask you a few questions about your business. This is when you begin the discovery process or business evaluation.

Ask questions to discover what their goals are and what's keeping them from accomplishing them. This will set you apart from all the other people they meet, especially other associates who's just trying to sell stuff. By showing this level of interest in them and their business you will establish a Big Brand Presence and help you develop rapport with the business owner. It's been said, "no one cares how much you know until they know how much you care." Invest the time to get to know them personally and to understand their business, what they do, and who their ideal client prospect is. Bob Burg, in his book "Endless Referrals" shared, "the more interested you are, the more interesting you become." Ask questions and listen. You will discover a lot about your prospects, their business, and you will build a lot of rapport.

During your interview, you might ask them where they would like their business to be in the next 12 months. Spend time understanding this goal and what it would do for them and their business to accomplish it. Then ask them what might be slowing them down, standing in their way, or blocking them from accomplishing it. Those challenges are the challenges you will need to solve with the Biz Plan. If they can't think of any challenges, ask them where in their business do they feel out of control. This deep question will yield some tremendous insight into their business. Once you know these two things, their goals and challenges, you have all the information you need to get them started as your new client.

You are a problem solver. Through the Biz Plans, you can help them solve problems they're having accomplishing their goals, and you can help them overcome challenges. Discovering their needs in doing these two things will allow you to offer solutions through the Biz Plans. The better you understand where the business owner is coming from, what they're trying to accomplish and what challenges they're having accomplishing these things, the better you will be able to share a solution.

One thing I've discovered is people are more inclined to act to avoid a consequence they would prefer to avoid than they are inclined to act to accomplish a goal. During the interview process, while it's important to understand the business owner's goals, a significant amount of time should be spent understanding their challenges and what impact those challenges are having on the business owner and their business. Try to discover the cost their challenges are having on them and their business. Work to get the business owner to give you a dollar amount when possible. This helps the business owner to more easily see the value of the Biz Plan when you share the solution. The greater the cost of the challenges the more the Biz Plan makes sense to the business owner by helping them accomplish their goals and overcome their challenges faster and cheaper than they could on their own.

This business evaluation element and the information you're able to discover through it, is critical to successfully getting a business owner started with the business plan. Once you get them started with the service, the things you discover during this step creates the starting point with your new client to help them grow and protect their business.

When I'm coaching new associates in the CORE Community on their presentations, often they share they spoke to a business owner and could not get them started. When I ask, what were the business owner's needs? Often associates can't tell me why the person they presented to needed the service. They were just sharing Features and Benefits. Consequently, the business owner did not purchase. Remember, people buy solutions. In order to share a solution during the presentation which will get the business owner to become a new client, you must understand their needs. You must show them how you can help to solve their specific challenges. Once you understand their needs, you can move with your prospect to the next compartment, or step, and close the door behind you.

GETTING THEM STARTED

The last part of the sales funnel is getting them started. If you've spent the time to discover their goals and what might be holding them back from accomplishing them, you have everything you need to get them started. Keep in mind, if they have not accomplished their goals, something is holding them back. If not, they would have already accomplished the goal and it would no longer be a goal, it would be their reality. Always keep in mind you're a problem solver and during the business evaluation they have just shared their greatest challenges they are experiencing in their business right now. The problem that's keeping them up at night and preventing them from reaching their goals. An associate doesn't get a new client started by throwing up a canned commercial, putting them into their autoresponder, giving them a tool, or sending to a video on their hub site. They get them started by sharing the specific signature solution which will solve their challenge and allow them to move forward to their goals.

As you share the solution to the business owner's challenges, the business owner is making the list I talked about earlier. The, I need that, but I don't need that lists. When the list of, "I don't need that" gets bigger than the list of things they need, you've lost the sale. For this reason, share specifically how the Biz Plan with GoSmallBiz add-on, or the SmallBIz Plan, is going to help them overcome their challenges and/or reach their goals. That's it, and get them started right there on the spot.

Think about it. They have a challenge which is preventing them from moving their business forward, probably costing them hundreds of dollars a month, or more, in actual business expenses or lost sales and income. It is wasting hours and hours of their time, causing them stress and frustration, and you've got a solution for $160 a month or less. It's a no brainer. Pull out your apps and get them started so you can start helping them utilize the service to solve the challenges or accomplish their goals quicker and easier than they could on their own! It really is that simple.

This is your authority amplifier and what sets you apart from other associates. You have solutions! AND you have their next steps, the next steps to take to solve their challenges and accomplish their goals. This moves you and your prospect from point A through this simple process, the CORE Method, to point B, a new client and a nice commission check on a clear path to success. How you think about this step, what you believe, whether you believe you can get them started on the spot or not will determine, more than anything else, your success in getting business owners started effectively.

I was working with an associate by the name of Dan. Dan was struggling to get business owners started right on the spot. So, I asked Dan a few questions. First, I asked if he was following the CORE Method script. He said he was. I asked him if he was doing an effective job of discovering the business owner's needs. He said he was. I asked him if he thought he was doing a good job of following the CORE Method of sharing a solution. Again, he said he was. I said, how about closing the sale. Were you following the script? And once again he said he was. I then asked him, "Dan, let me ask you. If I were to present this to you, would you need to think about it or would you purchase right on the spot." Almost immediately he said, "I would have to think about it." It was his belief that he would have to think about it. Because it was his belief, he believed everyone would feel the same way. Even though he was following the CORE Method and the scripts, he was giving each business owner the opportunity to think about it. This was killing his profits and reducing his closing ratios. Once we identified the problem, Dan changed his thinking. Instead of approaching the sales presentation with the thought of why would they buy on the spot, he approached it with the thought why wouldn't they. Of course they are going to get started at the end of my presentation, why wouldn't they. They have a challenge and I have a solution, it's a perfect match. Once he made this slight change in his thought process, his on the spot closing ratios changed and he began closing more people right on the spot.

Keep a close eye on what you're saying AND how you're saying it to make sure you achieve the goals you're trying to accomplish. Remember, you're transferring your beliefs. Make sure you believe the correct things to get the outcomes you want in your business.

MOMENTUM

And now the final step in our three-step process, building momentum and scaling your business to consistent income, consistently qualifying for Performance Club, the corporate trips, and getting started earning full-time income.

SOLUTIONS AND RESULTS

The first part of building momentum is all about doing what you said you were going to do at the time of sale, providing solutions and helping your clients get results. Remember, you're the problem solver and your new clients are not accustomed to using this kind of service.

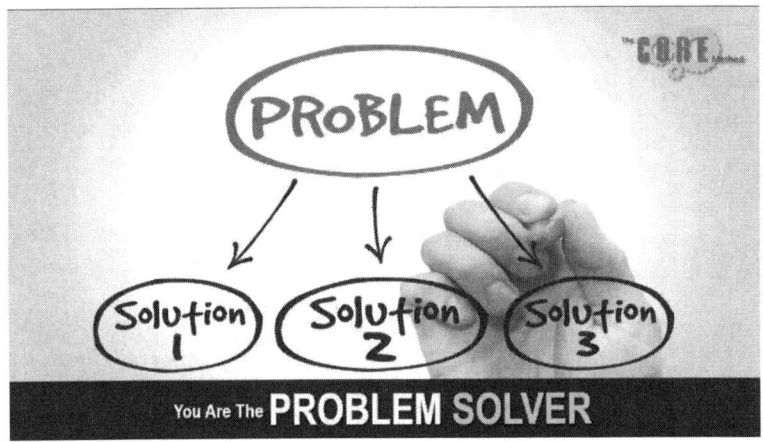

You should be back in your new client's business within a few business days from the time you signed them up to help them get started working to overcome their challenges and accomplish their goals. Usually, you won't know the outcome of whatever action you helped them take at the time of your visit. For example; if you got them logged into their GoSmallBIz Back office to submit a question, you won't know the answer to that question for a day or so. You will need to follow up again in a few days to check on the response. If you helped them call the law firm, it's unlikely the law firm will call them back while you're there. Again, you will have to follow up in a day or so to see what the response was. In many cases another question or another call will be required to give the business owner clarity and a path forward. Work with them to achieve this clarity of the next steps they should take. Each time you follow up and you help them utilize the service you're bringing value to your client and you're teaching them to utilize the service. Once you solve the challenge or help them accomplish their goal, you should sit down with them and discover what their next goal is and what might be holding them back from accomplishing it. This will keep you on a track of progression with your business owners and will keep them utilizing the membership. You should follow up with your clients on a regular basis to make sure they are using the service, **_and it is helping them_** overcome their challenges and accomplishing their goals. In other words, making sure your clients are receiving value from their membership.

Keep in mind business owner's purchase what they need for their businesses. If you don't follow up with your clients, help them and teach them to use the service, they won't use it. If they don't use it, eventually when looking over their bank statements or financials prepared by their accountant and see that monthly expense for the service they aren't using, they will cancel and you will suffer a charge back. That charge back is nothing compared to the loss of income you will suffer by not having the client anymore and losing the opportunity to get referrals from them to additional sales.

Over the years, as we were being recognized as National Top Producers, other Top Producers came and went. I remember one couple who were from Michigan and became Top Producers. They had gone on the road and traveled the country adding new clients. The problem was they didn't put this part of working with your clients and help them solve their challenges and get results through the Biz Plan as part of their business model. What occurred was their memberships started canceling off because the business owners weren't using the service and not getting value from their purchase. They ended up struggling to market enough memberships to cover their chargebacks, and eventually they quit the business. Make sure you follow up with your clients on a regular basis.

During your evaluation process, you discovered what the business owner needed and this was the basis for them purchasing the service. As their servicing rep, it's up to you to follow up with your clients and make sure they are getting solutions to the challenges they purchased the membership for. Don't rely on the Traditional Retention letters, emails, or calls to do this for you. Keep in mind, most business owners have never had access to this kind of service before. Traditionally, they waited until they had a challenge to speak to an attorney. Now they can proactively utilize an attorney to guide them in their business. They have probably never utilized a business consultant, so they don't think to submit questions. These are things you will need to train and teach your clients to do, starting with the specific challenges they purchased the membership for.

Once they overcome these challenges and accomplish their goals they purchased the membership for, you should sit down with them and rediscover what their new goal is and what is keeping them from accomplishing it. Then help them utilize the members to achieve this goal and overcome the new challenges. By working with your clients through this cycle you will help them utilize the membership, bring tremendous value to them. This will create raving fans of your clients and they will be happy to share all the business owners they know with you, which takes us to the next part of the momentum process, Referral Acquisition.

REFERRAL ACQUISITION

Referral acquisition is the next part of the Momentum step and the most critical of all the parts of this system. The entire system is designed to facilitate the acquisition of referrals. Without this one part, you cannot scale your business, accomplish momentum, or create consistent predictable income. This one part is the difference between an associate at the top of the leader board and the ones at the bottom.

You see, most associates are taught through the Traditional Training to prospect in their marketplace by making a list, following their dollar, and walking their community. However, there is little or no mention of profitability, consistent income, or scaling their business, just massive activity. As they do these activities they put prospects into their sales funnel. This takes time and money. When a prospect drops out the bottom of their sale funnel as a new client, instead of asking for a referral, they go right back to their prospecting venues or activities which costs them more time and money. They do this over, and over, and over again, struggling for their next sale. This is not how you market biz plans effectively and make consistent income, and it won't allow you to scale your business.

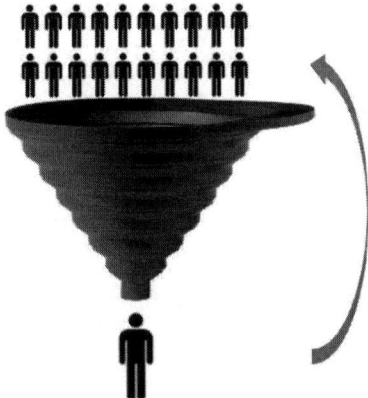

When the prospect drops out of the sales funnel as a new client, you must be able to get referrals. By doing this you invert the sales funnel and instead of a prospecting 20 to get 1 new client, you can get 5 or 6 referrals from your new client which should close at a 50% or greater closing ratio. Because you can go directly to your next sale through referrals and not have to go back to your prospecting venues, the sales process is shortened. This also reduces your costs of acquiring a new client, and allows you to quickly scale your business and generate consistent income.

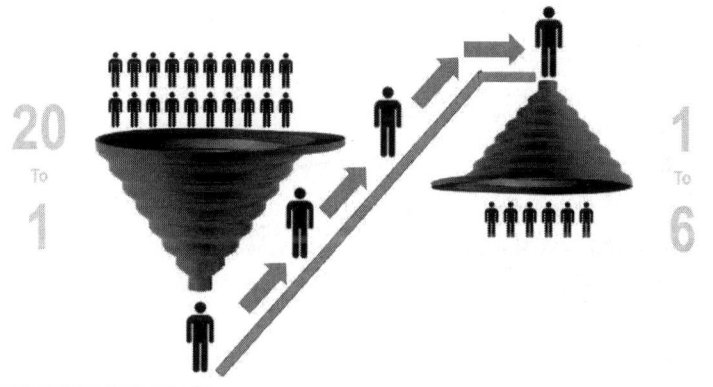

This one piece of the puzzle, missing from the Traditional Training, prevents most associates from consistent income and successfully marketing biz plans. It's the difference between a Top Producer and the average associate marketing a few Biz Plans a year and struggling to make their next.

Referrals should be obtained at the time of sale, and at each follow up. Mastering this part of the momentum process will transform your business. However, remember it starts at the beginning with the selection of the right prospects.

Timing is everything when asking for referrals. Make acquiring referrals part of your closing/application process. This makes referrals something you need to finish the paperwork and conclude your business, instead of something you would like the business owner to help you out with at the end of the paperwork process. If you wait until after all the applications are filled out and all the paperwork is done to get referrals, you won't get them. The business owner will say, let me think about it and I will give you referrals when you come back. It will never happen. By making it part of the application process you will leave with referrals more often than not.

You should utilize a professional looking form which allows the business owner to simply fill in the blanks to provide you with referrals. Without the form, how is the business owner going to give you referrals?

As I said, you should also get referrals on your follow ups. Once you have followed up and serviced your account, or stopped by to see how things are going, pull out your referral form and a pen and ask your business owner who they know who "**might**" benefit from the services you provide and the relationship we have? And wait for them to give you a name and number. Then ask, is there anyone else you can think of off the top of your head who "**might**" benefit from our services and the relationship we have? And wait for a name and a number. By going back to your marketing research, you can look at who they either purchase from or sell to and ask for a specific type of business. You might ask them who do they use for their uniforms for example, or who provides their raw materials and so on. You might ask them who they know who owns the same kind of business they have. Most people know lots of other people within their industry. If you have selected your business correctly from the beginning, they know people. Bob Burg in his book, "Endless Referrals" shared that most people know at least 250 people. When you return to follow up and help the business owner utilize the service, you're bringing them value and you should be able to get more referrals.

Once you get referrals from your clients, look them over and use the same criteria you used in your market research and organize your referrals to give you the best chance of success and your greatest profits. Look to see who they are, what their needs might be, who they purchase from, who they sell to. Organize your referrals to make best use of this information to shorten your sales cycle.

Once you have your referrals organized you want to go into their business, ask for the person you were referred to and share you were referred by (the person referring) over at (name of the business). I'm working with them and they thought what I was helping them with might be something you and your company would benefit from. Do you have a couple of minutes to see if that's the case? And start your Business Evaluation process and then move them to getting started and acquire referrals.

The two most important take aways of this book are, 1) Features and benefits don't sell, solutions do, and 2) Referrals are the only way to scale your business and generate consistent, predictable income. Understanding these two things and utilizing them in your business to guide everything you do will help you get your business to consistent full-time income.

BUILDING CLIENTELE

The last part of the momentum step is building clientele. This is where you scale your business. At this stage of the CORE Method you're transitioning from prospecting venues you participate in to build your base of clients to total referral based marketing, and it's as simple as 1, 2, 3.

1) Work through prospecting venues to get your business started, add individual clients, and obtain referrals from each new client.
2) Service these clients to provide an excellent client experience, help them accomplish their goals and overcome their challenges, bring value to them, and get more referrals on each follow up. Doing this allows you to grow your business and build momentum as you increase your bank of referrals and add new clients.
3) As your client base and referral bank grows you're able to transition out of your prospecting venues where you're investing a lot of time and money to generate individual sales. You can focus your time following up and working with your existing clients who in turn give you more referrals. This allows you to effectively and profitably expand your client base through referral based marketing.

When all your new clients are coming entirely from referrals you're getting from your existing clients, you've achieved momentum and have **Broken Free** to generate consistent income at a full-time level. Taking you from point A to point B through a logical progression that makes sense…The CORE Method.

The average associate never makes this transition. Because of their adherence to the Traditional Training, they spend their time working their prospecting venues making one off sales. Because they are not taught the importance of target marketing an ideal prospect they are not working with who will be the most likely to get started and provide them with referrals to their next sale. They are stuck in a downward cycle of spending time and money always trying to find their next client and never able to Break Free to the full-time income level.

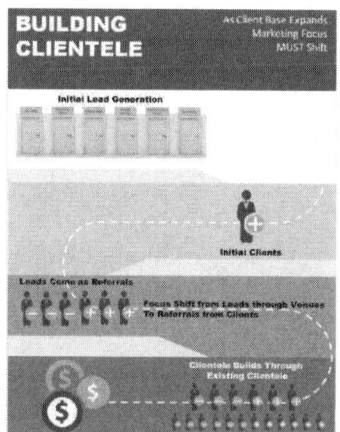

By applying the information in this book, you can start building a base of clients who purchase the Biz Plan with GoSmallBiz add-on or SmallBiz Plan, utilize the plan so they're raving fans of yours, and share their contacts with you so you build your sales and commissions to the full-time income level.

THE FLOODGATES

Let me share how you can open the floodgates to success by building a team of associates marketing Biz Plans. Let me give you a 30,000-foot overview of how this can be accomplished. The information I about to share with you is going to be total opposite from Traditional Training. However, after being a part of this industry and studying it for many years, a new more effective approach is needed.

Based on the Traditional Training an associate is taught to recruit anyone and everyone who is willing to join your business. It's often been said, "A Dud will lead to a Stud". However, this method ignores all the principles of a successful business and profitability. Remember, at the beginning of this book when I said everyone else has step-by-step paths to success. Training, certifying, on the job training, and so on. Everyone but direct sales reps. There is typically a Success Guide and a Next Step process. However, much of what the average recruit needs to be successful is missing. Key elements like I've shared in this book. The Traditional Training teaches a sink or swim approach to building a business.

The sink or swim approach to building your business is to recruit anyone and everyone you can, slam them into the business, get them a copy of the Success Guide, encourage them to take whatever training is available, again the training which is missing key elements. Once they've done this, get them plugged into the team and corporate conference calls, weekly briefings and events, and let them go. You've probably experienced this in your business. It is survival of the fittest. Some will sink and quit, and hopefully at some point you find someone that can swim and starts building, at least they do initially. In most cases, after they recruit a few people who can't swim they give up and also quit the business. However, there is a much better way and one that nearly guarantees the success of your recruits.

Imagine when you have implemented the CORE Method of marketing Biz Plans and you're adding new clients to your business on a consistent basis. As you add on new clients and get referrals you will build a bank of referrals as your client base grows. When you want to add a new client, you go to your bank of referrals, select your best referral from your bank, go visit the referral, conduct a business evaluation, get them started and get more referrals. When all your sales are coming from the referrals you have in hand and continue to get from your client base…you're generating consistent full-time income. You are nearing the flow stage of the 6-Figure Roadmap.

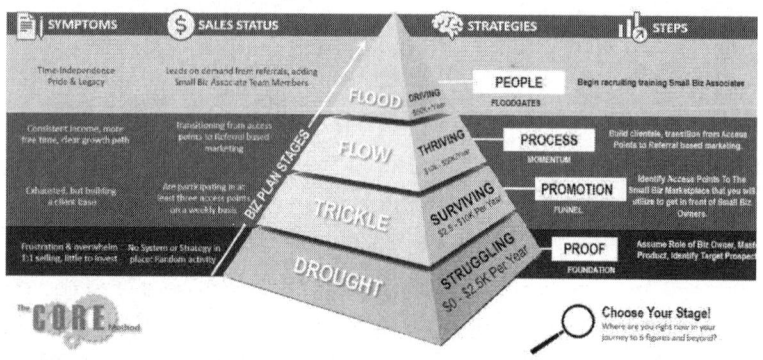

To move your business beyond this level and to the Flood Stage of the 6-Figure Roadmap and open the floodgates of income into your business you will need to bring on associates to help you market Biz Plans.

Because you've already done the work to build your business to a consistent income, you know how many Biz Plans you're adding each week. Because you've already built a bank of referrals you are drawing your new clients from, which grows each time you add new clients or do a follow up, you know this consistent income will continue. Because of this stable income, you could recruit new associates, use your bank of referrals to take these new associates under your wing and field train to continue to generate consistent sales. While those new associates are field training you could run those sales through their business, allowing them to get paid while field training and you to get paid through the override you generate from each sale. The new referrals you acquire during this field training process could be given to your new recruit to help them build their bank of referrals, so they can also generate consistent income. You have your own bank of referrals, so you don't need those. You need up and running associates much more. Once you are confident the associate is fully trained and ready to work on their own, turn them loose to build their business and generate consistent income for themselves and you will receive override income. Think about the possibilities and how much more effective this approach is to the sink or swim approach.

Now take this one step further. The quality of a person you recruit changes dramatically. Because you are confident of the income a recruit would be earning while field training, the increase in commissions they would earn as they put in sales, and the amount of money they could potentially earn, you can focus your recruiting efforts on professionals with existing sales skills.

Imagine what that would look like in terms of override income you would earn each time you brought on a new business partner. Now imagine how many people out in the world you could help right now with this business and recruiting model. Based on the examples I've used in this book, you know the income opportunity for yourself and every Biz Plan focused associate you recruit. You can check your comp charts and do the math. As I write this book, a Director overrides about $100 on every Biz Plan 50 with GoSmallBiz add-on, or SmallBiz Plan Pro a Manager sells. Let me ask you how many managers would you like on your team marketing Biz Plans? It's all available to you by mastering the information I've shared in this book and then recruiting people you can help get started using this method in their business.

As you can see there is a clear path from point A to point B, a clear path to success through all stages of the 6-Figure Roadmap which I teach in my CORE Method Training and Support Program to members of my CORE Method Community.

BREAKING FREE OF A TOTAL STATE OF TRAINING OVERWHELM

Breaking Free is all about winning at marketing Biz Plans and SmallBiz Plans. It's about helping you get started accomplishing a level of production you have control over which allows you to accomplish the consistent, predictable full-time income you've always wanted from your business.

When we were actively working the in the field, we had such high confidence we would be making a sale each day by adding a new client that we took a UPS envelope with a shipping label on it with us in the field each day. We were able to achieve the consistent income which allowed us to work our business while our kids were in school, being done by the time they finished. It was a dream come true for us and it can be for you also.

Let me show you how to go from a total state of training overwhelm where you're sitting there trying to figure out who to listen to. Everyone giving you just one piece of the puzzle. Everyone presenting themselves as self-proclaimed "B2B" or "Biz Plan" Experts. But, they haven't made consistent full-time income marketing biz plans. Everyone teaching you the Traditional Training, to go walk your community, follow your dollar, make a list, and get tools in the marketplace, but no one is having consistent success at it. Because as I have shared previously, those things don't work to generate consistent income. The truth is most people can't do those things successfully and that's not how top producers are generating consistent income.

You no longer have to go out and test and tweak trying to figure it all out. You no longer have to wonder who to talk to, what to say to them once you meet them, or how to make a sale. Instead, let's talk about how to turn your marketing strategy from a slot machine approach, where you put money in having no idea if you're going to get money out, and usually coming up short, to a marketing strategy which works like an ATM machine where you can get a logical, predictable outcome.

Think about what it would mean for your business if you had a strategy where you took specific steps and you got predictable results each time. How would that change your business and your income? If you knew each time you took three simple steps in your business, you get a new client and generate a $375 to $400 commission as a Director. How often would you take those three steps? That's what I'm going to show you how to do using the information I've shared with you in this book.

It's not about massive activity. It's about the right activity, in the right order, done consistently, as I have been sharing with you throughout this book.

1) Build your solid foundation
    a. Assume the role of a business owner and work for profits in your business.
    b. Master your product on a practical application level so you can share solutions to help your prospects accomplish their goals and overcome their challenges.
    c. Focus on the right ideal client prospect who has a need for the service, where you have access to the business owner, and who can lead you to other businesses.
2) Put your sales funnel in place
    a. Focus on lead generation venues which will give you access to your ideal client prospects on a consistent basis.
    b. Schedule appointments with those ideal client prospects in their businesses and ask questions to determine their goals and challenges.
    c. Share how the Biz Plan with GoSmallBiz add-on or the SmallBiz Plan can help them overcome their challenges and accomplish their goals quicker and cheaper than they could on their own.
3) Build Momentum

a. Work with you clients to help them accomplish results in their business.
   b. Get referrals from your clients which will lead you to other clients, allowing you to scale your business and earn consistent income.
   c. Transition from the prospecting venues you used to build your client base to total referral base marketing, working with your clients and getting referrals from them to new client prospects.
4) Open the Floodgates
   a. Building a team of professionals who are marketing Biz Plans as a full-time career opportunity.

I understand this approach is total opposite of what you've been taught during your Traditional Training, and what you hear in Facebook groups and even on Corporate Conference calls. But, remember, those Traditional Training methods are for them, the masses, the average associates, and they generate an average result. They are not for you, the associate who aspires for success in their business. They are for them, the masses, who they are trying to get to do something, anything to move them one step forward and generate a sale or a new recruit. They are not for you, the associate who is willing to learn and implement proven strategies which will allow you to quickly scale your business and generate the consistent, predictable full-time income you desire.

Back in 1966, the Founder of Amway Rich DeVos gave a speech at the National Junior Achiever Conference entitled, "Selling America." This amazing speech is as relevant today as it was back then. In this speech, he shared a conversation he had with a college professor. In the conversation they were debating business techniques. After listening to the professor for a few minutes he shared with the professor what he was sharing was not theory, it was fact gained from years of experience, data, and results to back it up. I share this because what I've shared with you in this book is not theory. It didn't come from a text book or a training manual. It came from actual field work marketing Biz Plans at a full-time consistent predictable income level to gain the experience necessary to write this book and create the training and support programs I offer today. Through the journey I shared in this book I was able to compile the data and obtain the results which allows me to share this proven system. You can choose to follow the outdated and ineffective Traditional Training, or you can implement what has been tested and proven to produce results at a full-time income level.

You can choose to continue to do what you've been doing, or start down a clear path to the success like you've been looking for. The choice is yours and yours alone.

HOW TO WIN AT THIS

Congratulations for choosing the clear path to get started down. Let's look at how you can implement this strategy in your business, the CORE Method, get questions answered, and see how you can win at this and make this happen for you and your business. I'm going to share how you can quickly implement the CORE Method, scale your business, and go from zero to consistent full-time income and beyond. Some of you may already be at that level but don't have this strategy in place for your business, and that's fine. I work with Ring Earners who are working to increase their income and scale their business. You can use this system to further increase your income and generate it more consistently. However, most of you reading this book are looking for some way to get started and cut out 90% of the wasted time, money, and guess work. So, how can you get there 5 to 10 times faster? You're looking for a system you can use which will provide you predictable, nearly guaranteed results. To increase your odds of success as much as possible right out of the gate. If you're still with me, still reading this book, what I've shown you so far makes sense to you. It's logical and you can see how by moving through this system, the CORE Method, you can get to where you would like to be. So, here's where it's going to get very interesting. Let me share with you what it takes to win at this fast.

I want to ask you, "Where are you right now with leads and sales"? My father told me a long time ago, there's two things you need to be successful when traveling anywhere in the world. You need to know where you're at right now and the exact destination you're trying to get to.

Think the last time you went to the shopping mall and you were looking for a specific store. You went up to the mall directory and did two things, right? You looked for the store you wanted to get to and then you looked for the "YOU ARE HERE" designation on the map. Knowing these two points, you were able to find the quickest way to get to where you wanted to go. But, when it comes to business, most associates don't have either of these things figured out and that's why they're struggling. We use a tool called the 6-Figure Roadmap in the CORE Method Community to guide us from where we are to where we want to be financially.

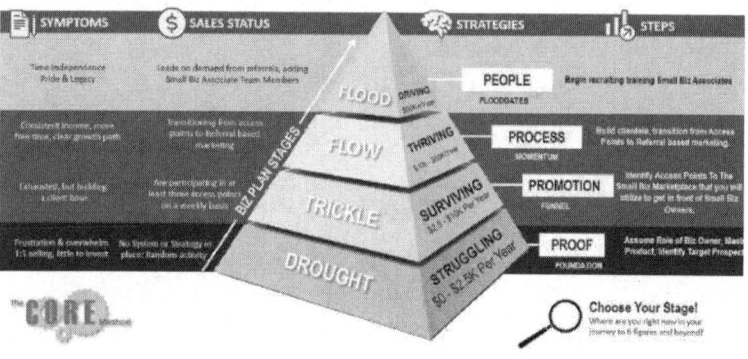

I'm not going to walk you through every bit of detail here. But I want you to understand where you're now, so I can show you exactly how to get to the next level. This is very important because these are the exact four stages every single associate goes through on their journey from zero to six figures and beyond. Literally, you're either struggling right now where you have a drought of leads and sales and generating between zero and $2,500 a year or you're surviving where you have a trickle of leads and sales and generating $2,500 to $10,000 per year in commissions. You might be thriving where there's a flow of leads and sales and you're generating between $10,000 to $50,000 per year, or, hopefully driving your business where there's a flood of leads and sales and you've reached the $50,000 income level or above.

Now for each stage there are different symptoms. You must know where you are and the status of your sales and income. So, if you have no plan or strategy in place, or maybe you have some inconsistent method you're doing, you're probably at the drought or trickle stage. You might have a system where if you just put more time and money into it you get increased results, you might be at the trickle or flow stages. Now the important take away for you, and the reason why I'm asking these questions, is depending on where you're at there's one key take away or strategy you need to focus on to get you to the next level and you need to stop doing everything else. This is the information diet I talked to you about at the beginning of this book. I want you to think about where you are in the six-figure road map and I'm going to show you how to get to the very next level.

What I know with absolute certainty is you're going to get stuck along the way. Everyone does. You reach those hurdles or obstacles which were small mole hills, but can become mountains of friction in your business. You might not know how to apply one of the strategies or tactics I've shared in this book to your specific activity or circumstances. You might be stuck on one thing you can't get over. You might even have a psychological impedance like not having the confidence or wherewithal to go ahead and execute a specific tactic or strategy. Let's be honest and real, everyone gets stuck along the way.

One of the biggest discoveries I made which has helped me and the CORE Method Community members is you need a success environment. This is very, very important and not stuff you hear elsewhere. But the thing is, this is how you get results.

Over the past 30 years of working in business, I've always had someone I could council with, talk through challenges I was having, and like Napoleon Hill said, "Create a mastermind where two brains form a third more powerful brain." Just being able to talk to someone who is supportive, who can coach you or brainstorm with you is so powerful and has remained the key factor in my success over the years.

Of the training programs I've invested in over the years, the programs I've had the most success with create a success environment for their students. These success environments always include these four elements to ensure the participants successful:

1) Ongoing mentoring and coaching
2) An accountability system to support implementation
3) Peer support
4) Systems, Frameworks, and Re-Enforcement Training

I use a framework called a MAPS environment to create a success environment for my CORE Method Community Members. It's very simple, very powerful, and effective in helping members move forward so they don't get stuck along the way. In fact, what I discovered was nearly every successful business owner or Entrepreneur you'll ever encounter uses these elements in some form or another. This is the secret no one is talking about when it comes to finding success. Let me walk you through them and I want to show you how to put these into practice in your business.

MENTORSHIP

Are you following someone who's achieved the results you aim to achieve? It's that simple. Have you attached yourself to a trusted advisor who knows what you should be doing in the specific area you're trying to have success in so you can cut out 90% of the wasted time and money you're spending trying to figure it all out?

One of the greatest pitfalls I see associates fall into is when they plug into traditional conference calls, Facebook groups, Traditional Training, or begin working with other associates who don't have the actual experience to help move them forward in their business. They spend countless hours doing activity which has very little hope of getting the ultimate results they are trying to reach. Often driven by hype and excitement, the Traditional methods are more designed to retain associates in their specific call, group, or training rather than provide them with a measurable result. Always make sure the person you're following is qualified to lead you to your desired result.

ACCOUNTABILITY

The world is full of information overwhelm and overload where there are so many competing forces for our attention and our time. The one catalyst for success which stands above all others is being accountable to yourself and others for doing that one thing which will move your business forward. You have to make sure you're doing the one thing a day, or a week which is going to produce the results you're looking for, which will move you one step closer to your goal.

The key to accountability is being accountable for the correct action or activity. In Traditional Training, you're encouraged to get a workout partner. Often these workout partners are associates trying to figure it all out also. What happens is that everyone involved in this accountability system is guessing as to what step needs to be done next and when it should be done by.

By plugging into a system with an accountability program built in, you follow the proven steps that work, decide how long you need to complete the step, and commit to move to the next benchmark by a specific date. This eliminates all the guesswork and wasted time and money doing things which won't move you to where you want to go.

PEER SUPPORT

It's been said, and proven, you're the product of the five people you hang around with the most. Most will end up with the same average income and outcomes as those five people you're spending the most time with. The associate who wants to succeed in any area of their business needs to associate with likeminded individuals who are doing or working to do what you're trying to accomplish.

Many associates go to their weekly briefings, team events, and Super Saturdays and hang out with other average associates who are what I call, Spectators. They show up to everything and say they want success but never take the steps or the action necessary to make that happen. What I've noticed is the associates in that group are all nearly at the same pin level, income level, and suffering from the same symptoms which are preventing them from reaching their goals. Without realizing it, each is preventing the other from moving forward because everyone through their actions encourages the next to stay right where they are. Each one makes it okay for everyone else to be a spectator because everyone else is spectating.

It is vital for your success to be part of a group of people working in the same area as you want success in, who are moving forward in that area, not stagnate. Connect with them so through the peer support within that group, the same force that holds you back in one will propel you forward in another, and you naturally move forward with them.

I remember my daughter, when she was playing basketball would sometimes play up with older kids and sometimes play with kids her same age. When she played with kids her same age, she played well at that level. However, when she played up with the older kids, by association she played at the older kid level. It improved her game, not because of some sudden burst of skill, but through a sudden burst of association.

So, you need this in some form to support you and help you stay on track playing at the level you want to be successful and accomplish your goals.

SYSTEMS, FRAMEWORKS, and RE-ENFORCEMENT TRAINING

At the heart of the CORE Method lies a step-by-step business plan which includes one-page frameworks, scripts, and next step instructions to help you quickly get started and scale your business, which I've talked about throughout this book. You'll use these systems and frameworks to shorten your learning curve and help you quickly get started and scale your business because the system has already been created and put in place for you. You don't have to reinvent the wheel or come up with a brand new untested system you must build from scratch. It's already done for you. That's the beauty of Systems and Frameworks. All you must do is jump in and drive away so you can spend 100% of your time focused on results.

Every business should have this, and all successful ones do. As I mentioned earlier in this book, most other career and business paths out there have a specific system in place to take a person just starting to success. All other careers, except yours, until now. With a training program, system, and support program you're able to plug into, you have a path to run on which will take you from point A to point B faster and quicker than you could any other way.

So, the M. A. P. S. environment is your success environment. You need all these in some form. Whether you get this from me or someone else you must have this in place in your business to virtually guarantee your success if you're willing to do the work to make it happen.

But let me explain how I can help you achieve the results I've talked about in this book.

THE CORE METHOD

So far, we've covered a great deal in this book. You might be a little shell-shocked saying how I've changed the way you look at marketing Biz Plans, the order you should be doing things, the method, strategy or techniques you should be using to get you the best results. I hope you have a greater understanding success lies in your foundation, and you should be using systems and frameworks to save time and allow for duplication of your efforts. You now know what to do, and what not to do in terms of the information diet and avoiding information overwhelm. But I want to show you how I can help you scale your business quickly.

So, let's get growing with the CORE Method Community.

In this book, I've shared a ton of information. I've shared a clear path to help you get started moving towards consistent full-time income for virtually any associate regardless of availability, circumstances, or marketplace using the Foundation, the Sales Funnel, and Momentum steps. To succeed at this, an associate must do the right things, in the right order. It's kind of like the combination to a safe. If the combination is 1, 2, 3, dialing 3, 2, 1, won't open the safe. It works the exact same way in your business. But in most cases, it is not having all the numbers so you get stuck and don't know how to move forward.

The CORE Method Training and Support Program is a program I put together which puts everything into a simple step-by-step process to virtually guarantee your success if you're willing to show up and do the work. Yes, that's right, the work. There is no lasting success without it, I'm sorry to say. No true get rich quick program that will allow you a shortcut other than following a proven system that's already in place. That system must be designed from experience to help you shorten the learning curve and fast track your success by avoiding all the pitfalls any associate would experience trying to figure it out on their own. That requires previous experience at the full-time income level marketing Biz Plans. Theory doesn't cut it when you are trying to help others. It's not go take the hill and ignore the cannon. It's let me show you how I took the hill and eliminated the cannon.

I believe the CORE Method is the world's simplest and most effective training and coaching platform for associates who want to rapidly scale and grow their business marketing Biz Plans and SmallBIz Plans without all the training and information overwhelm. Let me start by sharing the training courses we have as part of this program which is just the first part of the CORE Method. We cover everything I've talked about in this book in detail. Every lesson has step-by-step training in small bit sized chunks, exercises to help you master the information. Badges and achievement recognition in our community so you know you're accomplishing what is needed to build the knowledge and skills to be successful at this, along with accountability and frameworks. You show up, do the work utilizing the frameworks, and you move forward to the next level. By the time you've completed the program you will have 10 new Biz Plan Clients and generating a predictable income from your efforts.

The training program is laid out as follows:

The Biz Plan Opportunity Lesson

In this lesson, you will discover the incredible opportunity available to you. You will discover the market potential and income opportunity you have marketing Biz Plans. Once you understand the need in the marketplace and income which is available to you helping business owners, you will probably be losing some sleep because of your excitement.

Roles and Mindset Lesson

In this lesson, you will discover all the roles you must play in your business and the mindset you must have to be successful marketing Biz Plans.

You will establish the specific goals you want to accomplish for your business. You will identify the starting point of where you are, and the destination you want to achieve on this leg of your business journey. This will help you create you plan of action, so you can accomplish what you are trying to achieve for you and your family.

You'll also discover different ways to stay focused and motivated on growing your business and accomplishing your goals regardless of what's going on around you.

Product Mastery Lesson

In this lesson, you will expand your understanding of the practical application of the Biz Plan. You will discover how the Biz Plan can be utilized in the everyday life of a business owner to help them accomplish their goals and overcome the challenges they face each day. This helps you expand your product knowledge so you're well prepared to offer solutions to help business owners accomplish their goals and overcome their specific challenges.

Having this level of practical knowledge will allow you to share solutions, which sell, instead of sharing features and benefits which do not.

Market Focus Lesson

This lesson breaks from Traditional Basic Training you have received elsewhere which teaches you to go out and through massive activity talk to every business owner, which costs you time and money, and exposes you to huge rejection. Instead, this lesson shares who your specific ideal client prospect should be, so you can make best use of your time, get more business owners started, and make more money.

This lesson is vital to making a profit, scaling your business, and being successful marketing biz plans. Getting this wrong will doom your business.

Lead Generation Lesson

This lesson also breaks from Traditional Basic Training where you are taught to make a list, follow your dollar, and go walk your community. All these activities chew up your time and cost you money with ineffective activity and limited results. In this lesson, you will discover exactly where you can find your ideal client prospects you've identified in the previous lesson. Using the lead generation methods and scripts you will learn in this lesson, you can quickly schedule appointments with business owners who want to talk to you and learn what you have to offer.

Business Evaluation Lesson

In this lesson, you will discover how to conduct a business evaluation or business interview with a business owner, so you can discover what their goals and challenges are. To conduct this interview process effective, you will learn how to utilize, "Small Biz Meeting that Sells" interview framework. Using this framework, you will be able to discover everything you need to know to get a business owner started with the Biz Plan or SmallBiz Plan for long term use of the service.

Remember what I've said throughout this book? Features and Benefits don't sell, solutions do. That is a key takeaway from this book.

Without a system for discovering the business owner's goals and challenges, all you can do is share features and benefits in hopes they will see something of value. As I've shared previously, and you've probably already discovered, this is a time consuming, costly and ineffective method of sharing the biz plan to a business owner.

Getting Them Started

In this lesson, you will discover the exact framework, method, and script to close the sale and get a business owner started with the Biz Plan, often right on the spot.

All the lessons leading up to this one shares a logical progression the CORE method uses to move the prospect forward with you through the sales process. It allows you to build momentum with each step to get a positive conclusion from your meeting. By the time you get to this part of the sales process, so much momentum has been built in your favor it is difficult for the business owner to reverse course.

This process is specifically designed to guide the business owner through the sales process, so they come to their own conclusion they need what you have to offer. They realize the tremendous value for them, and you can help them accomplish their goals and overcome their challenges quicker, easier, and more cost effectively then they could on their own.

Solutions and Results Lessons

In this lesson, you will discover how client retention and new customer acquisition to work hand and hand to move your business forward. You will discover how to work with your clients, track your clients progress, and help them utilize the service effectively to accomplish their goals and overcome their challenges on a long-term basis.

In this lesson, you will also discover how to continue building the relationship you've started to a solid working relationship, and how to make additional money doing this.

Referral Acquisition Lesson

In this lesson, I share the most effective way to get referrals on an ongoing basis from your clients starting at the time of sale.

Getting referrals is one of the most important things you must do in your business and this strategy is key to your success. Without this one element, you will not be able to accomplish consistent income or scale your business.

Building Clientele Lesson

In this lesson, I share how to build a solid base of clients and scale your business to total referral based marketing. You will discover how and when to transition from your prospecting venues to total referral based marketing, spending all your time working with your existing clients and getting referrals. This will take you to the top of the flow stage in the 6-Figure Roadmap to the $50,000 income level.

These lessons are all part of the CORE Training Program. I don't offer these lessons individually. That's what the gurus do. They sell you on little pieces of the puzzle at each conference, special event, or training session, to keep you coming back. All the time you keep hoping you will eventually put it all together and start making money. This costs you money, wastes your time, limits your growth and income, and it doesn't fit into a greater strategy other than to retain you in the business for another 30, 60, or 90 days.

I'm going to tell you why I don't offer these lessons separately, and why you shouldn't be paying separately for each course. Because what you need is a clear path from point A to point B. Not a whole lot of content coming at you that costs you time and money and often only leads to more frustration. This is one of the challenges I have with the Gurus and leaders that push all the single pieces to the puzzle. They say you must go here to learn this, then you must attend this event to learn that, and don't forget to be at convention and sign up for all the breakout sessions so you can collect as many pieces of the puzzle as possible. It's seemingly endless.

The CORE Method training includes all the lessons I just mentioned and those lessons cover literally every step of the way. What I've done is taken all my 30 plus years of business experience, my experience of working in the field marketing Biz Plans, experience training and working with associates for over a decade, and put it all together in this one step-by-step program which takes you from zero to consistent income. If this sounds good to you so far, let me tell you how it all works.

It's literally time to say goodbye, starting right now, to all the frustration, stress, overwhelm and information overload for good…

It's time to say goodbye to paying tons of cash for all the endless trainings, events, and breakout sessions that only offer small pieces of the marketing puzzle, waste your time, and only cause you more frustration.

And most importantly, it's time to say goodbye to all the time away from your family and interests trying to figure out how the heck to duct tape all the training and information together to make it work and generate consistent income.

But, I do want to say, it's been my experience that old habits die hard. My question is when you wake up tomorrow, or next week, if you don't make a change today, where will your business be…your income be 90-days from now? I know I didn't have this kind of resource available to me when I got started. But this is the kind of resource I wish I had. So, I want to ask you, if there is any inkling, anything inside of you that thinks this might be a better, much clearer step-by-step logical path to follow to finally become more successful or reach a level of skill and income you want marketing Biz Plans, then I want to ask you if not today, when?

The first piece to the CORE Method is mentoring and coaching. We literally have LIVE video coaching available twice a week to help CORE Method members continue to progress forward in their business and get unstuck. It's very simple. You show up with your greatest challenge and I will get face-to-face with you, via LIVE video conference call, and help you get unstuck. I answer 100% of your questions. So, you show up for my LIVE coaching, you participate in our private community Facebook group so you're always plugged into what's happening and you can continue to move forward. The bottom line is I've taken all the guess work and all the friction out of growing your business and marketing Biz Plans.

The second piece is accountability. I have created a 9-step implementation and accountability program. Each step moves you forward one step, builds confidence and momentum, and once completed you will have added 10 new small biz clients to your business and generating predictable income. Each step is specifically designed to help you master the three steps of marketing biz plans I've covered in this book. You decide how long it will take you to master the step, set your deadline, and work to move forward on your specific schedule.

The third piece is peer support. Our community meets twice a week through LIVE video conference calls, supports one another, and learns from one another's accomplishments and struggles. You see and hear of the success which is occurring in the group and discover how to overcome challenges you may not have even experienced yet to help you avoid them in the future and fast track your success. The association in this group of go getters helps you play at a higher level than you would associating with the average associate.

The fourth piece is through our Systems, Frameworks, and Re-enforcement training. With Systems and Frameworks, you understand how to do each step and what is coming next. Re-enforcement training to help you continue to master and polish the skills required to make your business work.

I've created this success environment with Mentorship, Accountability, Peer Support, and Systems and Framework to create a turn-key, step-by-step program to fast track your success with predictable outcomes that allow you to scale your business fast. No guess work, and no hope marketing.

Whether you join the CORE Method Training and Support Program offered through the CORE Method Community or you find all these pieces somewhere else, this is what's required for success. For me, I had to go to piece all this together. However, I've put it all together for you in the CORE Method Community.

The system I've shared in this book works for virtually any associate regardless of whether you're working your business spare-time, part-time, or full-time. It works regardless of age, gender, or ethnicity, and it works regardless of your experience level. Simply put, this just works.

Now let me be totally direct. I don't know how much time you're investing in your business, or what you've already tried to generate consistent income. But let me ask you, what would need to happen for you to generate consistent income in your business doing what you're currently doing?

What is your confidence level with continuing to do what you've been doing? Will you get there in the next 6 to 12 months?

Now let me ask you, what would two or three biz plan sales a week do for your income level? What would it do for you and your family?

What is your confidence level that implementing this all-in-one, clear path to success, would work better than a bunch of training events, videos, and events without the exact steps, systems, and frameworks that don't fit together and are missing key pieces to the puzzle?

If your answer is you have a high confidence level these three steps, foundation, sales funnel, and momentum would work a lot better than what you've been doing, then you have a couple simple choices to make. How soon will you start implementing this information into your business? And, will you try to implement it on your own?

Now think about the cost of not taking action, of not implementing this information. Where will you be 30, 60, or 90 days from now if you don't do anything different?

I think you will have to agree if you look at what you're doing right now, and the clear path to success I've shared in this book, you would have to agree that marketing biz plans using this CORE Method just makes sense.

If you're interested in joining the CORE Method training and support program by becoming a CORE Method Community member, look for future emails when the CORE Method Community opens for new members. Several times a year, I open the community to new members on a limited basis. Because of the level of support we provide, we can only work with so many new community members at one time. For this reason, we limit the number of new members joining the community.

THE NEXT STEP

I have been asked more times than I can remember what's the secret to the success I've achieved over the years? They're often disappointed when I shared there is no secret. It comes from taking daily steps forward, Simple Daily Disciplines as Jim Rohn called them, which compounded over time allows you to reach your goals. It comes from executing these simple daily disciplines within a proven system which will allow you maximum results in the shortest amount of time. It comes from creating or joining a success environment where you are mentored by someone who's actually done what you are trying to do at the level you're trying to do it or beyond. It comes from being nurtured and supported by likeminded individuals working to get the same results you are within a system that works. But more importantly, it comes from you and your commitment to your own success and the results you can achieve.

I've explained throughout this book how it works with this one clear path to success system, the CORE Method. I encourage you to either join our community or find a community which will support you in like manner, step-by-step every inch of the way.

In the meantime, follow these steps to create success in your business:

1) Assume the role of a business owner

2) Study your products and learn them at a practical level
3) Focus on specific target prospects who will help you scale your business
4) Participate in lead generation venues to meet these ideal target prospects and schedule appointments at their business
5) Discover their goals and challenges
6) Present solutions to help them accomplish their goals and overcome their challenges
7) Work with your new clients to help them with solutions and achieve results
8) Get referrals from your clients
9) Build your clientele

If you add these 9 elements into your business correctly and with commitment, you will be on your way to the success you're working to accomplish in your business.

I know you can do it. I know you can accomplish your goals because I've done it and others who I have worked with over the years have done it. You are part of a minority, an exclusive group of associates who are willing to put in the time, effort, and energy to make their business a "Real" business. To **Break Free** from the Traditional Training model and average income associates earn from it, and accomplish the income you've always wanted.

You can be part of a revolution. A group of associates working to revive America by providing every day, main street America small business owners the resources they need to effectively grow and protect their business. You can be who others will look up to and aspire to as you build your solid business and get recognized for your accomplishments. But it takes work. It takes commitment to your goals and dreams, and it takes you moving outside your comfort zone where you are now competent to where you are not initially comfortable or competent. You see, you must move outside that comfort zone to where you're not comfortable and not competent so you can become comfortable and competent at an entirely new level. To where you can earn an income at an entirely new level. I challenge you to move to that place.

What I know to be true is you're currently making all the money you can make in your current comfort zone. To make more you must become more. You must learn new skills, you must become comfortable at a new level, competent at a new level. That's where your next income level is. That's were your dreams can begin to be realized. That's where you can help people the most. I challenge you to stretch yourself, push yourself to go there. The difference in your life, the life of your family, and the impact you will have to change the life of others will be worth the effort. In the greater scheme of things, when you look back from that place, you will be amazed at how quickly it happened for you.

I hope this book brings you value and success far beyond what I could have imaged for you. I look forward to hearing your success story and to see you at the top.

To your success,

- Charlie

Charlie Muhlenkamp, Founder
CORE Biz Systems